Justin Patten is a Solicitor and mediator, accredited by the Academy of Experts and founded Human Law in 2002. The firm covers Inheritance Disputes and Elderly Fraud claims.

Justin has authored 'A Practical Guide to Elderly Law' which was also published by Law Brief Publishing and has worked for Which? Legal, advising its members on elderly client issues.

A Practical Guide to Elderly Fraud

A Practical Guide to Elderly Fraud

Justin Patten, BA Hon, CPE
Solicitor, Accredited Mediator and
Principal at Human Law LLP

Law Brief Publishing

Published 2025 by Law Brief Publishing, an imprint of Law Brief Publishing Ltd
30 The Parks
Minehead
Somerset
TA24 8BT

www.lawbriefpublishing.com

Paperback: 978-1-916698-94-9

PREFACE

This book exposes the common misconception that financial abuse – including theft and fraud – is inflicted by individuals or organisations at arms-length, by people largely unknown to the victim. In fact a significant amount of financial abuse is inflicted by those much closer to home, namely family members. There is clear evidence that fraud is done by family members and the problem is understated within society. While many people are likely to be cared for with integrity by family members this is not always the case. This book seeks to cover the legal issues dealing with financial abuse and to help lawyers and other experts come up with practical solutions to help the people they work with.

It provides an introduction to set the scene, covers on conduct of elderly fraud cases and has a chapter on undue influence of wills, challenging the executor and the removal of executors. In addition, the book has chapters on will validity and fraud, undue influence of lifetime transactions, Part 64 proceedings and covers lasting powers of attorney, court of protection and deputyship fraud. At all points the book seeks to communicate in practical terms and to encourage the reader to think about positive and accessible solutions when helping those they represent.

The law is at 31st May 2025.

Justin Patten
June 2025

CONTENTS

CHAPTER ONE

INTRODUCTION

What Is the Primary Threat to Your Loved One's *Finances?*

It is famously said that sometimes the best hiding place is the one that's in plain sight.

Sadly, it is estimated that millions of older adults experience financial abuse each year, and the financial losses associated with this abuse can be devastating.

According to the Office for National Statistics, approximately 1.5mn older adults in England experienced some form of financial abuse in 2020.

As was pointed out by a report for Parliament by the All-Party Parliamentary Group (APPG) on Insurance and Financial Services and the Financial Vulnerability Taskforce

> *"It is a common misconception that financial abuse – including theft and fraud – is inflicted by individuals or organisations at arms-length, by people largely unknown to the victim. However, anecdotal evidence has for some time suggested that a significant amount of financial abuse is inflicted by those much closer to home, namely family members."*[1]

Professor Keith Brown, an Emeritus Professor at BU, who was a member of the Financial Vulnerability Taskforce and Chair of the Safeguarding Adult National Network, wrote the foreword to the report and observed:

---

1 https://80162760-26bc-4062-be5a-3322b8afa67b.filesusr.com/ugd/2c5374_1340b05c9a874b11adc0a3b24ed0aa69.pdf

> *"I constantly keep hearing cries for help from people who believe a family member has stolen funds from another family member, however there is simply no recent research or even debate about this issue."*

As the report observed it is worth noting that back in 2008, a report for Help the Aged stated that not only was 70% of financial abuse of older people perpetrated by family members, but it also estimated between 60 to 80% of these crimes took place in the home.

While theft and fraud within families is not restricted to older people, demographic changes including living longer will undoubtedly increase its prevalence, with property and complex financial resources a challenge for many to manage over time.

Thus we need to better understand the scale and nature of financial abuse in families. Only then can we move forward together to ensure it is both prevented and responded to effectively.

The lack of national research into theft and fraud within families has far reaching consequences across society.

If one does not understand the scale or nature of the problem, we are not able to identify and share best practice in prevention and action when it is believed to transpire.

There is clear evidence that fraud is done by family members and the problem is understated within society.

A 2015 survey by KPMG indicated a rise in the number of cases in which the perpetrator of the fraud was a family member.

While many people are likely to be cared for with integrity by family members this is not always the case.

One of the difficulties is this lack of awareness provided an environment for Elderly Fraud to thrive and often means that we are unable to deal with it.

Lasting Powers of Attorney is an arena for elderly fraud to take place

To give an Illustration of how legislators can make the wrong calls with respect to Elderly Fraud consider some legislation.

The Powers of Attorney Act 2023 makes changes to how lasting powers of attorney (LPAs) are made.

The Act aims to make the LPA process easier to access, simpler and apparently more secure from fraud and abuse.

Given many people do not think about LPAs until later on in life, it is often the elderly who find themselves the victims of identity fraud which is a key focus of the Act.

The changes include:

- Only permitting the donor to apply to register an LPA, removing the ability for attorneys to do so under the current rules.
- Enabling the parties to an LPA (the donor, attorney(s) or certificate provider) to choose whether to sign the LPA digitally or on paper, or by a combination of the two.
- Widening the group of people who can raise objections, including people not named in the LPA.

All well and good.

The LPA changes address such problems found out by an investigation by the BBC Radio 4 consumer programme, You and Yours who spoke to one victim whose empty home was targeted by fraudsters who obtained an LPA without any proper checks.

The fraudsters briefly visited the woman's home to change the locks and then tried to sell it using the LPA.

This has been a catalyst for the new law.

However the new Act once it is implemented will not actually address the real LPA fraud which is going on.

From my experience, nearly all the LPA fraud I see in my capacity as a lawyer is actually done by family members using a perfectly valid LPA document for which the elderly relative has often received legal advice.

None of the amendments within the new Power of Attorney Act will do anything to address this fraud because it will not increase the level of scrutiny of the LPAs in place.

With the rising numbers of LPAs(which the new legislation will lead to and increasing elderly population), this fraud will increase.

Most LPA fraud is not actually discovered until after the Donor of the LPA has died.

Then it is up to the Executor of the Deceased/Donor to investigate.

Most LPA fraud of this kind is not reported to the police and remains under the radar as far as the public is concerned.

If the fraud was reported to the police, the more likely response is that this is a civil matter.

An alternative course of action is to report this to the Office of Public Guardian (OPG).

The OPG has a legal duty to investigate complaints or concerns about the actions of deputies, registered attorneys and people acting under an order of the Court of Protection.

However, that legal duty ends when the deputyship/attorneyship ends which is when the Donor dies.

The only way the OPG can get involved after death is if you have a deputyship situation and they can get the deputy to produce a final report.

This does not apply to LPAs so it is really a case of a victim of financial abuse having to be very proactive after financial abuse has happened.

Thus contrary to media reporting(which focuses on scammers) and the view of society, the majority of elderly fraud is actually done by family members and/or those in position of trust.

Fraudsters Can Use Legal Documents

It is fair to say that much of elderly fraud is done by using illicit means such as iD theft, theft of bank cards.

In addition, types of financial abuse include :

- Taking money out of bank accounts
- Preventing a person from accessing their own money or assets
- Missing valuables from the home (e.g. jewellery, ornaments or art work)
- Deliberate isolation from friends and family
- Income missing or unaccounted for

- Suspicious payments to third parties

However, often what I term false friends/fraudsters use perfectly valid legal documents such as Lasting Powers of Attorneys and wills prepared by firms of solicitors to enact this fraud.

This step of "legalisation" makes both the fraud more difficult to detect but also more difficult to oppose once the facts come to light.

With respect to a will done by a firm of solicitors, it is actually fairly difficult to challenge that Will even if it has been masterminded by a false friend.

This can include a change of wills to favour certain individuals and misuse of a power of attorney or deputyship

From my experience, a number of people are fully aware of these vulnerabilities and have developed a well thought out and well implemented strategy which enables them to successfully obtain monies and assets from vulnerable people.

Until one has this thought in mind (and clearly our legislators and collective society have not), there will be a number of families who will be subject to elderly fraud and fighting an uphill battle to recover monies and obtain justice.

The purpose of this book is to shine light on this trend and provide you with the tools to both prevent you/your loved ones from experiencing this fate and also to give you the methods to fight back if it has already happened.

How is Elderly Fraud Done?

In order to have a full understanding of elderly fraud, it is necessary to fully recognise the (simple) strategy of committing the act(s).

Once you understand the primary way that most fraudsters/false friends commit elderly fraud you can develop your own strategies to minimise the risk of this happening.

In fact, there is actually a fairly simple strategy for committing elderly fraud as we do see it often with our work.

It consists of a Fraudster/False Friend doing the following:

- Exercising strong influence on a vulnerable person – manoeuvring the vulnerable person to give sole control (or effective control) of his or her assets to that bad person. This can be getting control of that person's financial affairs and if a Lasting Power of Attorney(LPA) is done, becoming a sole attorney.

- It can also involve becoming sole effective sole executor of the vulnerable person's Will. It is more difficult to challenge a will executed by a solicitor and despite safeguards this is relatively easy to do. Ironically the legal profession can be a very useful tool to enable a transfer of assets to manifest to a predator.

- Being both very self-serving and also, patient. Typically, other relatives (would be beneficiaries) under-estimate the lengths that the false friend will go to get what he or she wants. This puts the false friend at a fundamental advantage as they use any card possible to3 achieve their objectives.

- The false friend possesses good knowledge of the law. They know there are inherent weaknesses with the legal process which can be exploited. For example, it is difficult for other family members to challenge a Will prepared by solicitors. The individual knows that the Office of the Public Guardian(OPG, a possible safeguard) and indeed the police will be unlikely to intervene. As we will read later the OPG is not that effective in tackling elderly fraud as it is has a low successful enforcement rate.

Here are two examples of Elderly Fraud we have dealt with:

CASE STUDY 1

Jean lives in her house alone and is befriended by her nephew David and David moves into the property. David starts applying influence to Jean and Jean visits a firm of solicitors and changes her will making David executor and other family members beneficiaries. David stays in the property and takes hold of the Deceased's bank account and spends £100,000 of the bank account. He is eventually removed as Executor and leaves the country.

CASE STUDY 2

Dawn and Sheila are children of Alison. Shelia moves away from the area. Alison had done a joint will with the children's Deceased father which made Dawn and Sheila joint beneficiaries. Over time Dawn puts pressure on Sheila and gets her to do a number of wills which over a number years gradually increases the amount going to Dawn and also gives Dawn the sole right to be executor. Dawn takes hold of Sheila's bank account card and starts making ATM withdrawals and makes a series of payments to her and her husband.

Why are the Elderly Attractive Targets?

There are strong incentives to target elderly people.

The over 65s own £2.6 trillion worth of net housing wealth in addition to significant savings and investments, according to a report done by Savills.

If one is not doing that well economically the temptations to accumulate can be significant.

Older people are more likely to be vulnerable or have disabilities that make them dependent on others.

Some helpers may also have access to the homes and assets of these elderly people – including being able to remotely access their online banking and shopping apps.

Victims of such abuse are often reluctant to take action against their abusers because they feel ashamed of having been taken advantage of, or because they do not want the criminal to withdraw their care and support.

In addition, the criminal authorities will not necessarily get involved.

Individuals can mix the donors' assets with his, and so offsets his personal overdraft interest or props up an ailing business overdraft to assist short term cash flow.

Effective Implementation of Sanctions Against Fraud Weak

In an answer given in Parliament Mike Freer Finchley and Golders Green and the Secretary of State for Justice, responded to how many reported cases of fraud reported to the Office of the Public Guardian relating Power of Attorney were passed to the police or the CPS from the Office of the Public Guardian on the death of the alleged victim in the last five years.

The Office of the Public Guardian (OPG) has been recording data since April 2021 on concerns raised about Lasting Powers of Attorney (LPA) that mention fraud. Since April 2021, there have been 178 initial concerns that mention fraud. OPG carry out investigations following reports of fraud and act where they have the jurisdiction to do so.

From April 2019 to 31 October 2022, 15 fraudulently created LPAs were removed from the register following investigation. In 10 of these cases, the Public Guardian removed the LPA from the register. The Public Guardian referred the remaining 5 cases to the Court of Protection, which led to LPAs being subsequently removed. Fraudulent LPAs currently represent less than 0.1% of all registered LPAs, which exceed 6 million.

The OPG records the number of reported cases of fraud, but not the number that are passed to the police or the CPS on the death of an alleged victim. The OPG's legal authority ends upon the death of a donor (the individual who has created the LPA). As a result, where there is alleged fraud following the death of a donor, OPG would advise the concern raiser to raise their concern directly with the police if they feel it is appropriate.[2]

The number of referrals to police is low meaning that in a key area where elderly fraud can thrive(namely LPA) the chances of going to jail is low.

Examples of Fraud

However there are examples of fraud but these are a few.

Here is an example and the help given by a charity, Hourglass

Maria* was experiencing psychological and financial abuse at the hands of her son. He turned up at her property, demanding money and on one occasion took out a knife and threatened to kill himself if she didn't hand over £300.

2 https://questions-statements.parliament.uk/written-questions/detail/2022-1207/105551#:~:text=The%20OPG's%20legal%20authority%20ends,they%20feel%20it%20is%20appropriate.

Maria struggled to get over these experiences, and also felt lonely and isolated due to caring responsibilities. She rarely left home and felt like she was struggling to cope.

When Maria was referred to Hourglass, they matched her with a local volunteer who helped her re-connect with the local Portuguese community, as well as long-term befriending support. The volunteer also helped her claim welfare benefits, and gradually supported her in regaining self-confidence and independence. Without the support of her volunteer, Maria would have remained at home, with limited access to outside intervention and social opportunities to help with her recovery.

The service has been a turning point in her life and has enabled her to see past what happened and begin to enjoy her life once more.

Forging A Will

Mr Stewart Pearman was jailed for over five years for trying to steal more than £2 million left by a friend to an air ambulance charity before her death by cancer in 2016. He had been gifted £25,000 by his friend in her Will made in 2014 but shortly before her death forged a document that declared he was the sole executor and main beneficiary of her estate.

The two witnesses to the forged document initially gave evidence confirming that they witnessed the deceased signing the document but subsequently admitted that they signed the letter after the deceased had died.

In February 2023 he was sentenced to five years and three months at Worcester Crown Court.[3]

---

3 https://www.cps.gov.uk/cps/news/man-who-created-false-document-steal-ps2-million-air-ambulance-charity-jailed

The CPS brought charges against Pearman following an investigation by West Mercia Police.

In 2015, an elderly woman known to Pearman was diagnosed with terminal cancer and sadly passed away at her home on 7 August 2016.

The deceased wrote a will in 2014, making an air ambulance charity the main beneficiary of her estate. She left £25,000 to Pearman who she had appointed as one of the executors of her will.

Shortly after her death, Pearman produced a document which he titled 'Letter of Wishes' to solicitors dealing with her estate, declaring that he was now the sole executor of the will and the main beneficiary.

Pearman suddenly stood to inherit £2,186,079 - significantly more than the £25,000 which she had intended to leave to him in the 2014 will.

Solicitors appointed to process the will raised doubts about the legitimacy of the letter of wishes and an investigation was launched.

It was found that the defendant wrote the letter of wishes shortly before the deceased passed away, and medical evidence from the deceased's GP confirmed that she did not have mental capacity when the letter was purported to have been signed by her.

Pearman involved two further defendants Aleksander Yuriev Shikov, 35, and Luke William Derrett, 42, to support his criminal behaviour by requesting them to sign the letter of wishes as witnesses.

Shikov and Derrett provided sworn affidavits confirming that they signed the letter of wishes as witnesses after it was signed by the deceased.

However, they later confessed that they in fact signed the letter after the deceased had died.

Abuse of LPA

A man has been jailed for fleecing his elderly mother out her life savings of more than £250,000 while acting as her power of attorney.

The son of a woman with dementia who stole more than £250,000 from her to fund his luxurious lifestyle has been jailed.

Karl Zierold, from Stockport, was given power of attorney over his mother's financial affairs when her condition worsened and she was moved into a home.

Zierold, who was the eldest of four, was given full access to her bank account, draining it to fund holidays to Dubai and Mauritius, while also paying off his Mercedes V8 GT. His crimes were only brought to light when concerns were raised about an unpaid car bill.

When confronted the 56-year-old wrote letters to his family admitted he had stolen his mum's money. Jailing him for three years and four months at Manchester Crown Court Recorder Jason MacAdam said told him: "The phrase 'chip off the old block' is as far removed as can be possible when it comes to you."

They both pleaded guilty to wilfully making a false statement on oath and were s sentenced on 1 February 2023 to four months imprisonment suspended for 12 months.

Solicitors in the Dock

Elderly Fraud can involve an abuse of Professional Trust

There was solicitor who stole cash from a vulnerable client while acting for her under a lasting power of attorney (LPA) has been struck off.

The Solicitors Disciplinary Tribunal (SDT) heard that 38-year-old Danielle De Carpentier made 39 cashpoint withdrawals over nearly four years and totalling £7,850 from the client's personal bank account.

She was convicted of fraud by abuse of position in December 2021 at Nottingham Crown Court and later sentenced to 18 months in prison.

The Crown Court judge described her behaviour as "a gross breach of trust and abuse of position".

Her victim, 'Client A', was "a vulnerable lady, being unable herself to monitor her own finances, and thus there was nobody to operate as a check or balance upon your actions".

Once questions began to be raised, the judge said, Ms De Carpentier "embarked upon an attempt out of panic… to try and divert attention away from yourself but, in doing so, you sought to divert attention on to others, either real or imagined. That raised suspicion amongst others, none of which is edifying".

An agreed outcome with her regulatory body, the Solicitors Regulation Authority (SRA) and approved by the SDT, detailed that she began working for Clayton Mott in West Bridgford in June 2014 and, after qualifying as a solicitor in December 2017, she became a partner the following year. She left the firm in 2020.

The regulator said it received a report from Nottinghamshire Police in November 2019 that the solicitor had made the withdrawals of cash from various ATMs using Client A's debit card between August 2015 and June 2019.

A Call For Action

This book represents a call for action in making one aware of elderly fraud but also given one the tools to prevent elderly fraud happening in the first place and the tools to fight back.

One of the striking aspects of elderly fraud is the lengths to which family members are willing to plot and justify their obtaining of the elderly's assets.

This book by providing technical knowledge and practical solutions will provide you with the ability to prevail.

CHAPTER TWO

CONDUCT OF ELDERLY FRAUD CASES

TIP

An important fact to keep in mind is that Elderly Fraud case have a number of unique characteristics which we will cover below. One of the most important skills you can possess as a lawyer is an ability to detach yourself, obtain information, keep an open mind and not rush in such a case. Ultimately what you are trying to do is work out what has happened and then develop a game plan to help your client find the best possible solution.

At all points you should be humble enough to change course if the facts from your point of view change. An open minded, low key yet where necessary decisive mentality will serve you and your client well. We are specialists and our clients want us to act forcefully but we need to stay detached, calm and be open.

THE SEVEN INHERENT DIFFICULTIES OF ELDERLY LAW FRAUD CASES

1. COMPLEX – Elderly fraud cases can encompass situations which have happened over years and require significant financial information which is not always easy to discover and can even be time barred. Your client is unlikely to have unlimited resources so you need to be careful before jumping in and making serious allegations. You need to get an overview and ultimately work out what is important.

2. **EMOTIONAL** – As lawyers we are used to our clients being emotional but Elderly Fraud cases really do up the ante. You need to be careful about being sucked in to this and stay detached. The very nature of these kind of cases are fraught with intense emotions. As a consequence it is easy for your client and perhaps you as the lawyer to make a misstep. You need to be calm and think of long term objectives. In the face of provocative and sometimes emotional opponents and their lawyers, your calmness will serve you well and help you and your client if this matter goes to Court.

3. **COVER MULTIPLE LEGAL DISCIPLINES** – An Elderly Fraud case can involve a series of different legal arenas including criminal, inheritance, banking and civil law amongst others. Even within these parameters there are a number of possible legal steps that you can take and some of them can be time consuming and expensive. You may need to obtain legal support as and when and/or do your research. The selection of the legal steps is a critical skill.

4. **VERY PSYHCOLOGICAL** – With elderly fraud cases there is a lot going on beneath the surface. You do not need to understand precisely why but if there is client or oppositional behaviour which does not apparently make sense there may be reasons for this. By way of example, motivations of parties within Inheritance and Elderly Fraud cases can stem from issues related to childhood.

5. **STRONG FINANCIAL EMPHASIS** – Given that we are dealing with allegations of fraud one of the issues we face is management of financial transactions. This poses issues on obtaining those financial transactions and identifying anything illicit that has gone on a and then presenting the information. This is not necessarily an easy thing to do and an important skill set.

TIP

Use of money arguments. Particularly when you are dealing with a Judge, how you present information is a critical skill for proving illegal conduct. One of the key skills is to be succinct with the information and highlight clearly alleged financial impropriety.

6. CAN RUN AND RUN – Due to the wide nature of elderly fraud cases and the emotions you can find yourself in a situation where even a case has come to an apparent conclusion your client wants to keep going even when it is clear that they should not. For example, you win on a removal of executor case but there is still some money outstanding and the client is looking to obtain these monies elsewhere or seeks to enforce costs when it is not viable.

7. POSE PRESENTATIONAL DEMANDS WITH THE JUDGE – Even though this is a book about elderly fraud it is worth bearing that judges from our experience do not look like the term fraud and do not like you making these allegations.

TIP

One of the biggest errors that we see from barristers and solicitors is the tendency to use the fraud against others.

This can manifest in pre-action correspondence or in Appearance documents when one is lodging a Caveat. We will briefly cover Fraudulent Calumny elsewhere but even in the face of strong evidence be very careful how you put allegations of illegality.

A PRACTICAL GUIDE TO DEALING WITH ELDERLY FRAUD CASES

Keep an Open Mind

Evaluate Your Dispute (and Consistently Do So). Due to the emotional nature of elderly fraud disputes and the fact that as a beneficiary you often have limited information, it is very easy to misinterpret what the Executor is up to and to make poor judgment calls as to what are the strengths and weaknesses of a case and what you should do. Effective evaluation comes from consistent probing and a willingness to look at all available facts and ask searching questions of your situation. When we advise on a dispute what we are looking to do is to develop what we call a "Helicopter view" which means, rather than getting sucked into the detail of the case, we are seeking to find a clear and calm overview and help you understand how we think your situation will play out.

Some questions to ask –

- What evidence is there that something untoward has happened?
- To what extent are my views of this matter clouded by my emotions?
- Am I taking a fair stance in making steps to resolve this problem?
- How does any evidence stack up?
- Is there missing evidence I need to have a full picture?
- How will a judge see this if this did go to Court?
- What are my legal and negotiation options?
- What are the costs / benefits of the different options I can take?

- What are the specific legal costs which can be incurred?

Obtain as Much Key Evidence As You Can and Seek to Present It Compellingly

The nature of being in an inheritance dispute is there can be a lot of information which is not within your current knowledge. This can include evidence of the Deceased such as bank statements, medical records and other financial information.

A key skill which can make a significant difference to long term outcomes is the ability to obtain useful (possibly pivotal) evidence which you should be able to do at low cost. The more the beneficiary does this prior to instructing the lawyer the better the outcome. Also we are being honest here but the factual material within inheritance disputes can be, dare we say it, both unnecessarily long and boring. Not only is this potentially expensive for the beneficiary but is an expense which can be avoided. Thus, mastery of evidence and an ability to present this in a compelling and interesting way is a skill which can not only save time and cost in helping your lawyer be informed but also can influence the other side and a Judge.

Keep Emotions In Check

The nature of inheritance disputes often contains family history, and this makes it easy to make overly emotional decisions in dealing with your inheritance problem. This can lead to poor judgment calls and making rash decisions which can hurt you later such as making a judge unimpressed with your conduct. How you (and your solicitor) behave can be a critical component of how successful you will be if the matter goes to Court. Generally, in the face of provocation it will serve your interests to be calmer and it help you and your lawyer make better.

TIP

The term "Keep Emotions in Check" is watchword not just for you but primarily your client. Even in the face of strong evidence of elderly fraud it is very easy for our clients to damage their cases(possibly fatally) by even one misstep such as an errant email or a meeting which goes wrong. It is important for you to keep a close eye on your client behaviour and to manage your PR.

When can make this difficult is what we see as an increasing tendency of clients to think their views trump your experience.

Narrow The Issues.

From experience we find on elderly fraud case we find a lot of information emerges and sometimes a number of issues emerge. Despite the client pressure to argue points what your objective is to narrow the issues of dispute and not expand them. This helps you keep control of the case.

On elderly fraud cases what I am always trying to do is to identify the core issues (typically no more than five or six) and then focus on these.

Make Thoughtful Open Offers

One of the most important skills a solicitor can make is to make tactical offers which may go before the Court. Traditionally lawyers like to make solely Without Prejudice offers which are not seen by the Judge until after the main issue is determined at Court. I am a firm believer that where you are dealing with an inheritance dispute you should try to put as much as pressure as possible on the opponents by making offers to resolve your inheritance case which you want the Judge to see if the matter goes to Court.(e.g. highlighting your reasonable approach). For an example, even on fraud cases you should be seeking to explore mechanisms to narrow issues. Such an approach can lead to costs awards being awarded in your favour and protecting your client financially.

Select Negotiation and Legal Methods Carefully

As we have demonstrated when you have inheritance problems there are often in fact a number of legal and tactical options which you can use.

Sometimes errors can be made about which is the best method to select. It can be very tempting to jump in to what on the surface looks an appealing option when in fact what you should do is take a different course. The key step which will enable you to make a better decision is doing the Evaluation process thoroughly and then trying to work out what legal and negotiation step is going to get you where you want to be given your situation. That requires good background knowledge of legal and negotiation steps within this arena and an open mind.

Keep In Mind CPR for Negotiation

The Civil Rules state the following:

> Settlement and ADR[4]
>
> **8.** Litigation should be a last resort. As part of a relevant pre-action protocol or this Practice Direction, the parties should consider whether negotiation or some other form of ADR might enable them to settle their dispute without commencing proceedings.

4 https://www.justice.gov.uk/courts/procedure-rules/civil/rules/pd_pre-action_conduct#:~:text=Settlement%20and%20ADR,-8.&text=As%20part%20of%20a%20relevant,their%20dispute%20without%20commencing%20proceedings.

9. Parties should continue to consider the possibility of reaching a settlement at all times, including after proceedings have been started. Part 36 offers may be made before proceedings are issued.

10. Parties may negotiate to settle a dispute or may use a form of ADR including—

(a) mediation, a third party facilitating a resolution;

(b) arbitration, a third party deciding the dispute;

(c) early neutral evaluation, a third party giving an informed opinion on the dispute; and

(d) Ombudsmen schemes.

(Information on mediation and other forms of ADR is available in the Jackson ADR Handbook (available from Oxford University Press) or at—

https://www.gov.uk/guidance/a-guide-to-civil-mediation

11. If proceedings are issued, the parties may be required by the court to provide evidence that ADR has been considered. A party's silence in response to an invitation to participate or a refusal to participate in ADR might be considered unreasonable by the court and could lead to the court ordering that party to pay additional court costs.

Within elderly fraud cases you can use mediation and explore other ADR tools.

In my view, this helps your PR.

Explore All ADR Methods

One example of ADR is Early neutral evaluation (ENE) is where the parties appoint a neutral third party to give an expert opinion on the probable outcome of the case or particular aspects of the case. The evaluator will usually be a lawyer or an expert in the field and ENE can take place outside of or within the court process. For example, this can be a barrister.

You can arrange ENE yourself or you can see if a Court offers this.

ENE is offered in the Chancery Division by all judges and if it is unsuccessful the judge that undertook ENE will have no further involvement in the case (unless the parties agree otherwise). ENE is usually without prejudice. The opinion of the evaluator is generally non-binding unless the parties agree it should be binding. The evaluator will be more interventionist than a mediator. Instead of acting as a go-between to the parties, the evaluator will state what they think the correct decision is. This may assist in bringing about a settlement, especially if the parties are locked.

ENE is particularly suited to cases where the dispute turns on a point of law or construction.

In the Chancery Guide it states: 'Although ENE may be unsuitable for multi-faceted complex claims, if a particular issue lies at the heart of the claim an opinion could help unlock the dispute in a way which a mediator cannot. It is particularly suitable where the claim turns on an issue of construction, an issue of law where there are conflicting authorities...'

In 2019 in Lomax v Lomax,[5] the Court of Appeal held that ENE can be ordered as part of the case management function of the court and the

5 Lomax v Lomax [2019] EWCA Civ 1467

parties do not have to consent. The courts can order the parties to undertake ENE under CPR 3.1(m).

Think Outside The Box

With ADR you can always using barristers as a means to explore viewing documents. Below is part of a draft agreement that we used for attempting to settle a case and illustrates how ADR can be used on a case where as a beneficiary we sought access to bank statements which the Executor was not providing.

1. *The agreement is in full and final settlement of all and any claims and applications between the parties, and between your client and the estate.*

2. *Your client consents to the approval of the final estate accounts as per my clients' claim and agrees to the final distributions indicated by those accounts subject to the provision for litigation costs immediately below and any further administration expenses incurred.*

3. *Your client will bear her own costs including her costs of the claim, her application and intended Part 20 claim. My clients' costs of the claim, the application and the intended Part 20 claim will be borne by the estate subject to detailed assessment on the indemnity basis if not agreed.*

4. *My clients, through me, will provide to you (and for your eyes only) the bank statements for the deceased's bank accounts covering the period of the seven years up to the deceased's death. They will do so within 7 days of your confirmation for your client of the acceptance of these terms.*

5. *Neither the bank statements nor their contents are to be provided to, seen by, communicated to or in any other way shared with,*

your client or any third parties save, of course, that you are free to discuss them with me as my clients' legal representative should you wish to do so, and to state your position as to any inaccuracy in the IHT403 as below. The same confidentiality applies to any additional information which may be volunteered by my clients to you in connection with the accounts. Cheque stubs are not required.

6. *The purpose of the provision of such bank statements is for you to consider whether the contents of the form IHT403, identifying the gifts made by the deceased in the last 7 years of her life, are materially inaccurate - which means the omission of any gift or gifts amounting individually to £10,000 or more. Hence your analysis of the bank statements is confined only to those payments in the sum of £10,000 and above, and payments shown in the bank accounts of under £10,000 will, as you say, be ignored. Our clients will nonetheless, and for transparency, provide you with unredacted bank accounts for the 7-year period showing all payments, of whatever sum.*

If that disclosure does not demonstrate any material inaccuracy in the IHT403 (and 'demonstrate' for these purposes means as would be found by the court applying the civil standard of proof) then a consent order reflecting paragraphs 1 to 3 above shall be filed immediately. To that end those instructing you are invited to sign the attached draft Tomlin order by consent on behalf of your client to be held by my instructing solicitors on the strict basis that it is only to be filed upon your confirmation that the disclosure demonstrates no material inaccuracy in the form IHT403. Obviously we would appreciate it if your confirmation (or any queries you may have prior to that confirmation) be provided as soon as possible but in any event within 14 days of the receipt of the bank statements.

If you are unable to provide that confirmation then you are to identify any alleged inaccuracy and paragraphs 1 to 3 will only apply subject to determination (within the existing proceedings) of any remaining dispute between the parties as to whether or not there is any material inaccuracy in the IHT403 as alleged; and any correction of the estate accounts which may resulting from that alleged inaccuracy.

Litigate Smartly

This means your lawyer trying to retain maximum control and discipline within the litigation process. It requires the solicitor to be successfully and consistently evaluating your case and being discerning in using expert evidence (such as barristers and financial experts). We believe if you are going to use any legal process you have to be extremely careful in the forum you use so time and cost are not unnecessarily wasted especially as there are significant differences in the time frames / service delivery of the Court you can use. e.g. mediation with a good mediator and the High Court with electronic and prompt Court filing are dispute resolution methods we do support provided it is the best option for you at a given me. Litigate Smartly involves skilful wording in correspondence which has maximum influencing impact. Our firm offers clients fixed fees for litigation so we have every motivation to act in a disciplined way on your case.

Manage Cost

You have a professional duty to update your client on the costs position. A key skill is to maintain perspective and not get sucked into endless litigation which means the costs are completely unjustified.

Be Forensic But Not Boring

Within elderly fraud cases it is necessary to be restrained and factual and succinct. However, ensure that you keep your presentation interesting. After all you are trying to apply influence over the other side(their advisors) and ultimately the Judge.

TIP

Elderly fraud involve serious allegations

Keep yourself anonymous and maintain respect for the other Side. What you do not want to do is to is to make yourself a factor in the case. As a consequence(even in the face of provocation and possible pressure from your client), maintain a low key position.

APPENDIX Extract The Business and Property Courts of England & Wales Chancery Guide 2022

Early neutral evaluation ('ENE')

10.18 ENE is a simple, independent evaluation of the merits of a dispute or a particular issue, by a judge or someone with relevant expertise. This evaluation is non-binding and without prejudice unless the parties agree otherwise. It is given after time-limited consideration of core materials, the judge having read or listened to concise submissions.

10.19 The court may order ENE at a case management conference if it deems it appropriate. Following Lomax v Lomax [2019] EWCA Civ 1467, this may be ordered even if one or more party does not consent.

10.20 There is no one type of case which is suitable, though complex factual and legal disputes are generally unsuited to ENE. It can be particularly effective where the claim turns on an issue of interpretation or an issue of law, where the case involves the court forming an impression about infringement of intellectual property rights, or where the case is an appeal against a decision of a lower court, tribunal or office holder.

10.21 ENE may be provided by appropriate third parties or by the court pursuant to its powers under rule CPR 3.1(2)(m) of the Civil Procedure Rules ('CPR'). If it is provided by the court, the ENE will generally be conducted by a judge of the same level as would be allocated to hear the trial (or appeal), but the parties may agree otherwise.

10.22 There are no set procedures for ENE. The judge who is to conduct the ENE will give such directions for its preparation and conduct as they consider appropriate. The court will usually direct the parties to provide and exchange written position papers and to agree a bundle of core documents. The ENE can be on paper but in some cases the judge will direct a short hearing of up to half a day (2.5 hours).

10.23 Unless the parties have agreed that the ENE will be binding, the court will not retain on the court file any of the papers lodged for the ENE or a record of the judge's evaluation.

10.24 The judge conducting the ENE will have no further involvement with the claim unless both parties agree otherwise.

10.25 A draft ENE order can be found at Appendix K.

Chancery Financial Dispute Resolution ('Ch FDR')

10.26 Ch FDR is a form of ADR in which the court facilitates negotiations and may provide the parties with an opinion about the claim or elements of it. It is without prejudice and non-binding and will not be ordered unless all parties consent.

10.27 It is generally necessary for the parameters of the dispute to have crystallised before a Ch FDR takes place. This will generally not be before completion of statements of case or the exchange of evidence in a Part 8 claim.

10.28 However, if once acknowledgments of service have been filed, the parties consider that an early Ch FDR would be beneficial, they do not need to wait for the first hearing but can make an application using form N244. They should file a consent order substantially in the form to be found at Appendix L.

10.29 At all stages the parties should give careful consideration to what information may need to be exchanged in advance of any Ch FDR to facilitate any negotiations and enable the court to provide an opinion on the claim or particular issues. This may include agreeing to early limited disclosure or expert evidence (see paragraph 10.36). This is particularly important if the Ch FDR is to take place at an early stage.

10.30 The parties should consider who needs to participate in the Ch FDR to ensure it is effective. This includes ensuring all relevant decision makers are present and/or whether representation orders are necessary or appropriate and/or how different interests are to be represented at the Ch FDR.

10.31 If non-parties are to attend (by agreement between the parties) the parties should notify the court and seek permission by letter filed on the CE-File. Usually the court would expect this to be limited to, for example, a family member or close friend supporting a party to the claim. They would have to sign a confidentiality agreement.

10.32 However, if the parties consider it necessary for a non-party to be present for the purposes of the negotiations because they have an interest in or are necessary for any overall resolution of the dispute, but are not a party to the claim itself, consideration should be given to the need for them to sign a confidentiality agreement and/or what role they are to have at the Ch FDR. It may affect the terms and form of any agreement reached by the parties at the Ch FDR and how it is to be approved or implemented.

10.33 Ch FDR has been particularly effective in resolving disputes about shares in property, business partnerships, probate and inheritance.

10.34 Ch FDR will usually be undertaken in London by a Mast Master or an Insolvency and Companies Court Judge and in the B&PC District Registries by specialist B&PC District Judges, or where the case warrants it by a Section 9 Judge.

10.35 Ch FDR is a dynamic process. There will be a Ch FDR meeting in which the court plays the role of both facilitator and evaluator. Parties must be present at this meeting. The court will try to lead the parties to agree terms but will not make a determination. If the parties request it, the court may express an opinion about an issue or the claim as a whole.

10.36 In advance of the Ch FDR meeting the court will give directions which may include directing the parties to exchange and file without prejudice position papers (and direct what is to be addressed) and to lodge a bundle. If expert evidence is likely to be required or helpful for the Ch FDR, the court may permit that evidence to be filed and exchanged for the purposes of the Ch FDR without the need for a CPR compliant report.

10.37 The court will allocate time for initial discussions between the parties before the commencement of the Ch FDR meeting.

10.38 Unless the parties have agreed otherwise, the court will not retain on the court file any of the papers lodged for the Ch FDR or a record of the judge's opinion.

10.39 The judge conducting the Ch FDR will have no further involvement with the claim.

10.40 A draft Ch FDR order can be found at Appendix L.

CHAPTER THREE

UNDUE INFLUENCE OF WILLS

One of the most important elements of an elderly fraud claim can be to distinguish between undue influence of wills and undue influence of lifetime transactions as the legal position is strikingly different.

TIP

With undue influence of wills it is easy for you and your client to make a nuisance of yourself for low fees (It costs £3 to enter a caveat and you pay £3 to extend another six months at a time) and then ultimately placing an Appearance for no fee in assuming that a Warning is lodged.

This blocks probate and at the least causes inconvenience to the opposing side.

All well and good.

It is worth reflecting that proving Undue Influence is a different ball game and difficult to achieve and there are costs consequences if this does not work out.

While some lawyers like to aggressively make allegations of Unfair Influence (or go further and allege Fraudulent Calumny) conservatism is a better watchword.

There is a path to success of Unfair Influence of Wills but it is narrow and certainly involves careful management of the legal process and evidence.

It is worth having the manta inside to be cautious in conducting an unfair influence claim.

As was said in Re Cutcliffe (deceased) Le Duc v Veness [1958] 3 All ER 642 at 648–649:

> 'a plea of undue influence ought never to be put forward unless the party who pleads it has reasonable grounds upon which to support it.'

Overall dealing with the undue influence of wills is a narrow parameter and specifically difficult to prove.

Within wills it revolves around proof of coercion over the testator.

Sir James Hannen further defined undue influence in the context of probate in Wingrove v Wingrove (1885) as being "*To be undue influence in the eye of the law there must be – to sum it up in one word – coercion*".

In *Re: Edwards* [2007] EWHC 1119 (Ch); [2007] WTLR 1387 Lewison J, summed up the doctrine by references to how "*the testator's will must be overborne*", further to the exercise of "*pressure that overpowers the volition without convincing the testator's judgment. It is to be distinguished from mere persuasion, appeals to ties of affection or pity for future destitution, all of which are legitimate*" (at [47]).

The case of Brennan v Prior & Others [2013] EWHC 287(ch) illustrated that persuasion was due influence in which Ms Brennan challenged the will alleging undue influence by the siblings.

However, dismissing Ms Brennan's challenge, the judge said that evidence did not support her accusations of dishonesty; there was nothing irrational about the testator's bequests, and that while there "*is plenty of evidence that [his sisters] had the opportunity to influence [the testator] in the making of his will...I find persuasion but not coercion.*"

A party seeking successfully to challenge a Will must produce evidence of circumstances which leaves the Court not satisfied that, on the balance of probabilities, the testator understood its nature and effect, and sanctioned the dispositions it made. 14 [2017] EWHC 2559 (Ch) 14 As a matter of policy, the Court is cautious about accepting such challenges.

Wills frequently give rise to feelings of disappointment for would-be beneficiaries which can lead to contentions that the Will did not reflect the testator's true wishes.

A factor to have in mind is that if judges were too ready to accept such contentions the principle of testamentary freedom could be undermined.

Allegations that a beneficiary has engaged in this behaviour are not to be made lightly. Of course, the very nature of such conduct is that it is unlikely to have been publicly demonstrated.

As the authorities therefore recognise, it is possible for that reason to infer that coercion has occurred without there being any direct proof that it has: e.g. *Schrader* v. *Schrader* [2013] EWHC 466 (Ch); [2013] WTLR 701 (at [96]).

The burden on any Claimant to prove their case is high, despite the fact that the standard of proof is still only balance of probabilities.

In order to run a successful will challenge on the ground of undue influence, there must be sufficiently strong evidence that the testator was coerced to such an extent that the resulting will was not truly of the testator's making.

A Warning to Practitioners

Undue influence in a probate case will only rarely be proven. The whole notion of undue influence in the context hence requires lawyers and their clients to exercise degrees of cautious judgement.

These cases demonstrate that the surrounding circumstances are of the utmost importance in establishing undue influence. The following is a non-exhaustive list of potentially relevant factors:

Variables

- the testator's level of dependency on the influencer;
- the frequency and nature of the testator's contact with the influencer;
- the testator's personality and behaviour;
- the influencer's personality and behaviour;
- the testator's relationship with others, especially if the testator became more isolated;
- whether the will was a departure from earlier wills;
- whether a solicitor was involved in drafting the will; (*My view is that for a case of undue influence there is a world of difference between a home-made will as supposed to a will drawn up by a firm of solicitors.)*
- who contacted and communicated with the solicitor;
- how and what instructions were given in respect of the will.

TIP

Even if your legal matter looks like a compelling technical case for unfair influence it is critical that the actions and character of your client are sound.

You would be asking a lot of the Judge to back you in an unfair influence(or fraudulent calumny) action connected with a will.

As a lawyer you may wish to ask yourself – To what extent do I have sympathy for the client?

Sometimes your gut reaction will help you more than a detailed analysis of the case.

On unfair influence case everything has to be right; there is no latitude for errors.

The High Burden

Undue influence is rarely pleaded alone and will usually be pleaded alongside lack of testamentary capacity and want of knowledge and approval.

Knowledge and Approval With Wills, the testator must know and approve the contents of the Will (this is not applicable to a statutory will).

There are likely to be adverse cost consequences if allegations of undue influence are held to be unfounded by the court. This is possible even if the court finds a lack of testamentary capacity as undue influence is founded in fraud.

TIP: Beware on Costs on allegations of fraud or undue influence

- An allegation of undue influence or fraud ought never to be put forward unless the party who makes it has reasonable grounds on which to support it: *Mitchell v Gard* (1863) 3 Sw. & Tr. 78; *Spiers v English* [1907] P. 122

- Failure to establish such allegations will as a general rule be followed by condemnation in costs: *Summerell v Clements* (1862) 3 Sw. & Tr. 35; *Leo v Levy* (1909) 25 T.L.R. 717; *Re Cutcliffe* [1959] P. 6 CA.

- By alleging undue influence, a party takes on a significant costs risk; there is little prospect of costs being ordered out of the estate in a such a case.

Recent Case Law

Jones & Ors v Jones [2023] EWHC 1457 (Ch)

Background

Daphne Jones died in September 2021. She was survived by three of four children (her daughter Vicky died in February 2021) and eight grandchildren. She had made a will in July 2021 in favour of only one of her children, Ceri. She did not have any previous wills. The deceased had been diagnosed with early mixed dementia in 2020 but had lived independently at home until 2021, when Ceri went to stay with her.

The claimants were the deceased's surviving daughters, Catherine and Jacqueline, and the children of Vicky. They challenged the will on the basis of a lack of testamentary capacity, lack of knowledge and approval and undue influence.

While the deceased had a dementia diagnosis the judge was satisfied that there was no evidence that the deceased lacked testamentary capacity.

The judge also rejected the knowledge and approval claim, finding that the will, whilst homemade, was straightforward to follow and understand.

However, the judge found that the facts in this case pointed "*inevitably*" to the conclusion that Ceri did indeed coerce the deceased into making her will.

The judge listed ten reasons for reaching the decision:

1. There was evidence that Ceri believed she should inherit her mother's house, including text messages sent by her to other family members.

2. The deceased had always expressed her testamentary wishes to be equality between her children.

3. The judge was conscious the deceased would have been grieving the death of Vicky when she signed the will.

4. The judge heard evidence from various witnesses to the effect that the ability to make contact with the deceased became progressively harder after Ceri moved in with her, supporting a "*vivid picture of the deceased becoming increasingly isolated from them*".

5. Ceri reacted angrily when the deceased's brother tried to discuss the will with the deceased during her lifetime.

6. Ceri told the deceased deliberate untruths about the other family members.

7. The deceased was physically and mentally vulnerable and very dependent on Ceri when she signed the will.

8. Ceri denied being involved in the preparation of the will but there was evidence that she was.

9. The will was signed without any legal or medical professionals being involved.

10. Even after the will was signed, Ceri further distanced her mother from her family, friends, social workers and the police.

Conclusion

The judge concluded *"...Notwithstanding the high burden [of undue influence], I am satisfied that Mrs Jones signed her will not as a free agent, but because her volition had been overcome, without convincing her judgment, by the undue influence of Ceri Jones*".

The will was held to be invalid, and the deceased's estate passed on intestacy.

Rea v Rea [2024] EWCA Civ 169

This is a significant case which shows the inherent difficulty of running an unfair influence case.

The facts of Rea v Rea were Mrs Anna Rea died in July 2016. She was elderly and immobile, and relied on her daughter, Rita, and a carer, who lived with her, to help her day-to-day.

Her eyesight was not great, and she spent most of her time doing adult colouring books. She had made the contested will on 7 December 2015, and left her biggest asset by far, her house in Tooting, London, to her daughter, Rita, and the residuary estate in equal shares between her four children, Rita, and her three sons David, Nino and Remo.

This was very different from the previous will from 1986, which left the whole estate to the four children in equal shares.

The case had a long procedural history and took a number of years to be resolved. The EWCA established that the EWHC mistakenly found there to have been undue influence and the evidence provided did not entitle it to arrive at that conclusion. The EWCA ordered that the 2015 Will be admitted to probate.

This decision highlights that it is more difficult for disappointed beneficiaries to prove undue influence in such cases and there may be a presumption that there is no undue influence even if a beneficiary has persuaded a relative to change the terms of their Will.

The claimant then appealed to the EWCA. Her appeal was heard by Moylan LJ, Newey LJ and Arnold LJ, who have now published their unanimous decision that she had not been proved to have procured the making and execution of the will by undue influence.

Giving the judgment, the EWCA acknowledged that the claimant 'may have an argumentative and forceful personality, and [a] forceful physical presence' and had reason to seek to secure the property for herself. However, it also noted that the deceased had testamentary capacity and knew and approved of the terms of the will.

Moreover, it found that there was 'no direct evidence of coercion' and two experienced professionals with relevant expertise saw 'no reason to believe that there had been coercion'. They confirmed that the deceased had 'consistently expressed her wish' to leave the house to the claimant even when the latter was not present. She was also, they said, capable of rejecting suggestions from the claimant and of revising her instructions in the claimant's absence. Further, the court commented, 'there was a perfectly rational basis' for giving the claimant the property, as she had lived there and looked after the deceased for six years, whereas the deceased considered that the defendants 'did not care for her [and] had abandoned her'.

As Newey LJ put it: "it seems to me that it will commonly be appropriate to proceed on the basis that undue influence is inherently improbable. As I have said, "undue influence" signifies coercion in this context, and potential beneficiaries are surely less likely to resort to coercion than to rely on affection, gratitude or even persuasion". The court then went further, noting how: "the circumstances must be such that undue influence is more probable than any other hypothesis. If another possibility is just as likely, undue influence will not have been established."

The EWCA concluded that the EWHC was mistaken in finding there to have been undue influence and the evidence did not entitle it to arrive at that conclusion. The EWCA duly ordered the will to be admitted to probate.

You can win Undue Influence of Wills But This Is Against The Grain

In Harrison v Barrett [2023] (Case No: PT-2021-000349) a daughter successfully proved testamentary undue influence using the transcript from recordings on a camera, installed in the deceased's home, of conversations between one defendant and the deceased who was, at the time, suffering from dementia.

Evidently, this is not an option available for many claimants and the legal issues surrounding obtaining evidence in such a manner can be complex.

Mutual Wills Have a Different Test

However, in Naidoo v Barton [2023] EWHC 500 (Ch), a rare decision relating to the use of mutual wills, the High Court has overturned the surviving spouse's will on the ground of undue influence.

In this case, the confidence of Mrs Naidoo in her son's advice was sufficient for her to instruct for mutual wills to be drafted on the terms that David dictated. The benefit that David received from this decision far outweighed any benefit which Dr and Mrs Naidoo may have gained: "*The sole beneficiary of this restriction would be Mr Barton, who would be bound to take the estate of the survivor on death.*" Stating that "*there is no satisfactory explanation*" for the mutual wills on the part of Mrs Naidoo, the court concluded that such drafting could only have resulted from a measure of influence and subsequent unfair advantage taken by David.

The court determined that it is the *Etridge* test for undue influence, which applies to challenging life time transactions, (covered elsewhere) that applies when considering whether or not a mutual wills agreement should be set aside and not the more strict probate test that generally applies where a will is challenged on the grounds of undue influence.

TACTICS

Remember The Difficulty Newey LJ cited the usual cases about how the civil standard of proof works in respect of serious allegations, and held: "*it seems to me that it will commonly be appropriate to proceed on the basis that undue influence is inherently improbable. As I have said, "undue influence" signifies coercion in this context, and potential beneficiaries are surely less likely to resort to coercion than to rely on affection, gratitude or even persuasion.*" So there is a high standard of proof to meet, but in circumstances where direct evidence is usually in short supply.

Be Wary What You Are Alleging

It is often suggested that an allegation of coercion is tantamount to one of fraud. If so, that creates another obstacle: it is professional misconduct to allege fraud in the absence of *prima facie* evidence, so the claimant's representative may be professionally inhibited from pleading undue influence on the basis of only circumstantial evidence.

Path To Winning

There is a path to victory in cases like these but what you need to do is to focus on evidence that leans to proving undue influence and/or focusing on the negative character of the other party if you possess these facts and they are relevant . How you conduct yourself as an advocate is a relevant factor.

Fraudulent Calumny? Do you want to allege fraudulent calumny?

While this is a book about elderly fraud you need to be careful prior to making specific allegations of elderly fraud.

I err on the side of caution before using the word fraud.

There is a very high evidence threshold for proving fraudulent calumny.

In order to prove fraudulent calumny the court Will need to be satisfied of the following:

- False Statements: There must be evidence of false statements or misrepresentation made to the testator. This could involve lies about the character or intentions of a potential beneficiary.

- Impact on Testator: You must be able to show that these false statements had a significant impact on the testator's decision-making process. In other words, the testator must have been influenced by the misinformation in a way that led to changes in the Will, and that they would not have intended to make these changes if they had not been fed this misinformation.

- Intent: You must be to show be evidence of the perpetrator's intent to deceive the testator for their own benefit, or to the detriment of another potential beneficiary.

It is not enough to have a strong feeling or circumstantial evidence that the testator's mind has been poisoned against the potential beneficiary; you must be able to demonstrate that misinformation Will intentionally passed to the testator with the intention of having them change their Will.

Contesting a Will on the grounds of fraudulent calumny requires careful examination of the evidence and a thorough understanding of the circumstances surrounding the creation of the Will itself.

TIP

When I see an opponent allege fraudulent calumny I quietly smile to myself as in myself I know judges do not like these allegations unless there is compelling evidence. Do not allege fraudulent calumny unless you have real evidence and are willing to take it forward.

If I am opposing a lawyer who has made a spurious allegation of fraudulent calumny on behalf of someone, I will ensure that if the matter does go to Court the judge will know that allegation has been made.

A Successful Claim – Speakman v Muir[6]

In Speakman v Muir [2022], the court set aside three wills the deceased had made in quick succession in early 2018 on the grounds of fraudulent calumny.

The claimant was the deceased's son. The three wills had steadily reduced and eventually extinguished his entitlement to his father's estate; under previous wills, he had been due to receive half. The first defendant was the deceased's household assistant, and the deceased left valuable personal

---

6 Lexis Citation 1487 the High Court in Birmingham

items to her under the wills and substantial cash legacies to her granddaughters.

The latest will was accompanied by a note from the deceased explaining that he had excluded the Claimant from benefiting because Claimant had taken personal property from the deceased's previous residence and refused to return it. The Claimant had taken some items, but this was at the deceased's express invitation. The Claimant alleged that the First Defendant had poisoned the deceased's mind by telling him that Claimant was financially abusing him and had stolen items from him.

Although the judge found almost none of the witnesses wholly reliable, he focused on some striking contradictions in First Defendant's evidence. She said that her role in the wills' preparation was limited (and attempted to conceal it).

In fact, she had organised and attended meetings with the deceased and a will drafter and given them her contact details under the pretence she was the deceased's niece. She was also familiar with the contents of the wills, which did not align with a limited role in their preparation.

The judge observed that the deceased's physical and emotional vulnerability meant he was easily influenced by the First Defendant's domineering character and hostility towards the Claimant.

CHAPTER FOUR

CHALLENGING THE EXECUTOR

In the next two chapters we cover the steps that can be taken to deal with a fraudulent executor. It remains likely that that if you have what you believe is a fraudulent executor you will want to commence removal of executor proceedings which we do cover in depth in the next chapter.

However sometimes this option is not possible for certain reasons (e.g it is too costly, there is a disagreement between the beneficiaries or it may not be the right time.) Thus you need to be aware of your other options and to certainly consider them as a specific way to apply legal pressure on the Executor and to protect the assets of the Deceased.

How to Deal With Possibly Fraudulent Executors

An executor will generally remain entitled to a grant of probate and to administer the estate in priority to anyone else (Non-Contentious Probate Rules 1987).

If an executor is being difficult, what are tools are at his or her disposal to bring the executor into order? For ease of reference what we are referring to are options which lie if the deceased died in England and Wales.

TIP

The executor is given one year to distribute the estate – As a result during that year be cautious (unless there is a risk of assets being illegally distributed) in taking action.

However if you are in possession of credible allegations of fraud, we are looking at a different ball game and you may want to proceed more quickly.

But bear in mind be very careful how you put forward an allegation of fraud as it could have damaging consequences later.

At all points it is worth reminding an Executor the following:

An Executor has an obligation to gather in the assets, pay the liabilities, protect the estate and distribute to the beneficiaries. The fiduciary obligations include identifying debts owed to the estate. Lifetime transactions A residuary beneficiary will have standing to make enquiries in relation to lifetime transactions which impact upon their residuary interest. The standing to investigate vests with the Executor.

If a residuary beneficiary suspects that certain lifetime transactions made by the deceased should be set aside, they should request that the Executor obtain the relevant documents, eg bank statements, medical records, attorney accounts, etc.

The Executor and the beneficiaries should consider the requirements of the pre-action protocol and the Code of Conduct of the Association of Contentious Trust and Probate Specialists (ACTAPS) when considering how to cooperate and resolve disputes at an early stage.

Pre-grant

Where trouble arises or is anticipated, the following routes can be considered.[7]

Caveats

Often a sensible first step in stopping a grant of probate to an unsuitable executor is to enter a caveat, as it prevents a grant being made in respect of an estate (except grants ad colligenda bona or pendente lite). Indeed in some cases such as citations, a caveat is a necessary precursor.

The procedure is mostly contained in NCPR r.44. Unless warned, caveats generally remain in force for six months, unless the registrar orders otherwise but they can be extended for subsequent periods (see NCPR r.44(3)). Guidance is given online.[8]

What are Caveats?

Caveats are a system of preventing common form grants. They are important where there are genuine concerns about the validity of a Will or the suitability of a particular person acting as executor or administrator. The caveat procedure is used to prevent a Grant of Probate or Letters of Administration being taken out in respect of a deceased's estate. The person who puts the caveat in place is called the caveator.

Why would you want to lodge a caveat?

An excellent but dated article on dealing with executors is "Tackling troublesome executors" by Charlotte Black and Richard Sims, March 2009 which covers these issues in more depth – https://www.step.org/journal/step-journal-march-2009/tackling-troublesome-executors

8 https://www.gov.uk/stop-probate-application

The reasons include:

- Where the caveator wants to prevent the Grant of Probate being taken out as they believe the Will of the deceased is invalid for some reason, such as the person who made the Will did not have the mental capacity to do so, the Will was not properly witnessed or it is a fraudulent will;

- Where the caveator wants to prevent a Grant of Letters of Administration being taken out on the basis that the deceased died intestate, when they believe there was a validly-executed Will in existence; or

- Where the caveator is aware of or involved in a dispute about who is entitled, or is the appropriate party, to take out the Grant of Letters of Administration.

When is it not appropriate to issue a caveat?

It is not a good idea to lodge a caveat where the caveator wishes to bring a claim under the Inheritance (Provision for Family and Dependants) Act 1975. This is because a claim under this Act can only be brought once the grant of representation has been taken out. This is a common error made. However, it can be an inexpensive way to block estates.

What is the procedure for issuing a caveat?

If you're entering a caveat yourself, you can:

- apply online or by post

- make an appointment to visit a probate registry

You will need:

- the full name of the person who's died and any other names they were known by
- the exact date of death on the death certificate
- the last address of the person who's died
- your home address in England or Wales
- your email address (if you want to apply online)

If you do not have the death certificate

You can enter a caveat without the death certificate, but you must amend the caveat with the exact date of death when you know it. The probate application might not be stopped if the date of death is wrong.

It costs £3 to enter a caveat.

If you apply by post, you must pay by sending a cheque payable to 'HM Courts and Tribunals Service' with your form.

How can the caveat be removed?[9]

Caveats last for 6 months. They stop all applications for probate on the estate being granted during that time.

If the probate applicant disagrees with your caveat, they might:

- come to an agreement with you and ask you to withdraw the caveat

---

9 https://assets.publishing.service.gov.uk/government/uploads/system/uploads/attachment_data/file/905668/pa8-eng.pdf

- issue a formal 'warning'

Withdrawing or amending a caveat

You can withdraw or amend your caveat by email or post. In your email or letter, include:

- your 16-digit caveat reference
- the full name of the person who has died
- confirmation you want to withdraw the caveat or details of what needs changing

If you have responded to a formal warning by 'entering an appearance', you cannot withdraw your caveat. It can only be removed by order of a District Probate Registrar, High Court Judge or District Judge.

The caveator can remove the caveat at any time by writing to the Probate Registry. Given this a legal letter may be a good idea informing the individual that it is an abuse of proceedings to issue a Caveat inappropriately (see Parnall v Hurst [2003] WTLR 997.)

Any interested person may therefore issue a "warning" to the caveator. A warning is a notice to the caveator and must be in the prescribed form. A warning can only be entered at the Leeds District Probate Registry. There is no fee for issuing a warning to a caveat.

To give warning you need to:

1. Request a form from the Leeds District Probate Registry.
2. Fill in the form and say why you're entitled to apply for probate. This is known as stating your 'interest' in the estate.

3. Send the form back to Leeds District Probate Registry. The completed warning form will be recorded, dated, stamped with the court stamp and returned to you.

4. Make a copy of the warning to keep.

5. Send or give the warning to the person who entered the caveat. Keep a record of how and when the warning was given, for example, by hand or by post. You cannot give a warning by email.

The contact details are:

Leeds District Probate Registry
leedsdprenquiries@justice.gov.uk

Leeds District Probate Registry
York House
31 York Place
Leeds
LS1 2BA

The person issuing the warning must state the nature of his interest and the date of the Will (if any) in the warning and it must be served on the caveator in accordance with specific rules as to service. The warning must also require the caveator to state the nature of his interest.

Once the warning has been served on the caveator, one of the four things will happen depending on what right the caveator is alleging and what steps he chooses to take:

a) The caveator may withdraw his caveat – this can be done at anytime before he enters an appearance to the warning. When a warning has been issued, then the caveator must give notice of his withdrawal to the person issuing the warning. The caveat must be withdrawn at the registry in which it was entered. No fee is payable upon the withdrawal of the caveat.

b) The caveator may enter an "appearance" – an appearance should be entered in the prescribed form at the Leeds District Probate Registry within eight days of service of the warning on the caveator. If the caveator does not enter an appearance then the person issuing the warning may take steps to "warn off" the caveator. Once an appearance has been entered, the caveat remains in force until a District Judge (or, when the parties consent to the discontinuance of the caveat, a registrar) otherwise directs. There is no fee for entering an appearance.

c) The caveator may issue and serve a summons for directions – this must be done within eight days of service of the warning, otherwise the caveator risks being warned off. Please note that a summons for directions may only be issued by a caveator who has no interest contrary to that of the person issuing the warning. After a summons for directions has been issued there will be a hearing before a District Judge at which he will decide to whom a grant should be made.

d) A caveator may do nothing – in this case the person issuing the warning may file an affidavit in the Leeds District Probate registry after the eight-day time-limit for entering an appearance has expired. The affidavit must show that the warning was served on the caveator. The caveat is then said to be "warned off" and is no longer effective so that the person issuing the warning is then free to proceed with his application.

TIP

Caveats are an inexpensive blocking tool and can actually quite effective to bring the other side to the table. For this very reason they be the most appropriate method in a fraud case to delay the executor from accessing funds.

Be warned that your bluff may be called and then you have to be prepared otherwise your client will face a costs award. E.g In the case of Elliott v Simmonds [2016] EWHC 732 (Ch), the person who entered the caveat faced liabilities in excess of £100,000 after allowing her caveat to remain in place despite having all the documents which proved her will validity claim had no merit.

As we see later, they must be used if you are about to issue a citation.

Renunciation

Renunciation is only an option where a nominated executor is cooperative since the executor cannot be forced to renounce.

This can only be used where an executor has not already intermeddled with the estate.

Anyone named as an executor in a will may abandon the role by signing a renunciation witnessed by a disinterested witness, ie the witness must not be mentioned in the will, and should not be a family member.

Even in the case of a potentially fraudulent Estate, renunciation is an appealing option as you are taking power away from the Executor.

What is Intermeddling?

Intermeddling is carrying out the sort of tasks that an executor may do, such as letting a bank know of the death. If there are two executors and one is given a specific legacy and takes possession of that legacy without consent of the co-executor, this will amount to an act of administration.

Arranging a funeral is not intermeddling.

A renunciation must be absolute, and will take effect from the time that it is signed; though it remains possible to withdraw it at any time prior to it being lodged at the probate registry.

Once it has been lodged (together with the original will, or if this is not available, a verified copy), it can only be retracted with the permission of a district judge or registrar.

Where an executor is willing and able, however, for example where he simply wants nothing to do with the administration, he may renounce, effectively abandoning his right to a grant of probate (see AEA s.5(iii)).

This allows the next entitled person (under NCPR r.20 – generally a residuary legatee), to take a grant.

The renunciation must be in writing and while this can be done any time after a testator's death. Once made, a renunciation can be retracted but only with the leave of a district judge or registrar, and only in exceptional circumstances where probate has already been granted to someone else (NCPR r.37(3)).

Please see precedent.

Citations

Where renunciation is not possible, citations are a good tactical way of trying to force a delaying executor into action, or to entitle someone else to administer the estate.

There are two main types to consider: a citation to accept or refuse a grant, and a citation to take a grant.

Citation To Accept or Refuse a Grant

- Applies where an executor has not intermeddled and cannot be persuaded to renounce.
- Is taking no steps to obtain a grant of probate, he can be cited by the person next entitled to a grant to accept or refuse probate (NCPR r.47(1)).
- If the executor fails to appear or apply for a grant, the citor is entitled to apply for a grant to himself (NCPR r.47(5)(a); 47(7)(a)).

Citation To Take A Grant

- Applies where an executor has intermeddled in the estate (so that renunciation is impossible).
- Has not taken a grant within six months of death he may be cited by any person interested in the estate to show cause why he should not be ordered to take a grant (NCPR r.47(3)).
- If the executor fails to appear or apply for a grant, the citor may apply for an order requiring the executor to take a grant (if such an order is made and breached, the executor will be liable for committal), or for a grant to himself or someone else (NCPR r.47(5)(c); 47(7)(c)).

Before any citation is issued, a caveat must be entered in respect of the estate and no court fee applies.

TIP – Citations

Given the importance of fraud allegations it is unlikely that one would consider a citation application(why enable a potentially fraudulent executor to retain control) but if costs are limited and it is suspected the Executor will not react, it may be an option worth considering.

Procedure

A citation of any type may be issued by the Principal Registry or by a District Registry and must be settled by a District Judge or Registrar. (NCPR 1987 Rule 46 (1)). The application for the issue of a citation may be made in person or by post. Everyone with an interest in the document should be cited.

An affidavit should not be sworn before a citation is settled so that it can be corrected if it does not cover the required facts. Every Will or purported Will referred to in a citation must be filed.

A citation must be served personally unless otherwise directed (NCPR, Rule 46 (4)). A Certificate of Service should be endorsed.

A person who has been cited then enters an appearance at the Registry from which the citation is issued by lodging Form 5 to the NCPR.

The form sets out the name, address and interest claimed by the citor as shown on the citation. It should also give the full name, address and details of the interest of the citee himself including the date of the Will under which such interest arises.

The citee must serve a sealed copy of the appearance on the citor by delivering it at the citor's address for service or by sending it there by post or otherwise. The time for appearance is 8 days after service of the citation but it can be extended.

Passing over

Within the scope of s.116 of the Supreme Court Act 1981 the High Court may appoint someone other than a nominated executor (or any other entitled person) to administer the estate if it considers that by reason of any 'special circumstance' it would be 'necessary or expedient' to do so.

This can be over disputing co-executors, where there is a conflict of interest, and it can also be useful where the executor is thought to be of bad character, or where he is unlikely to administer the estate properly (such as in Re Biggs Estate [1966] 1 All ER 358).

The Court will take a broad view of "special circumstances" under s 116: Some other authority worth looking is re Clore decd [1982] Fam 113 (and on appeal as IRC v Stype Investments (Jersey) Ltd [1982] Ch 456) and Buchanan v Milton [1999] 2 FLR 844.

Generally the words "special circumstances" are not necessarily limited to circumstances in connection with the estate itself or its administration, but could extend to any other circumstances which the court thinks are relevant, which lead the court to think that it is necessary, or expedient, to pass over the executor.

The application is made without notice to the District Judge or registrar, with a supporting affidavit, (NCPR r.52), which must disclose all material facts to the court, otherwise the grant could be revoked (Shephard v Wheeler (2000) Times, 15 February).

Grant ad colligenda bona[10]

If the dispute looks set to continue on for some time, it is possible to consider an application for a grant ad colligenda bona defuncti.

This gives a limited grant of administration enabling the estate to be administered in the meantime for the purpose of preserving its assets.

A key aspect of a grant ad colligenda bona – and why it is attractive to the registrars and the court – is that it merely preserves, and does not allow for distribution of the estate as between competing legal parties.

It is often possible for both executors and beneficiaries to agree to this emergency measure, but it is not always an appropriate course of action, and can be an expensive and time-consuming process.

It should only be used where there is a genuine risk to the estate, and not merely to ensure a tactical advantage – see Ghafoor v Cliff [2006] 2 All ER 1079.

However, the judgment in Sifri v Clough & Willis [2007] WTLR 1453 was key of the professional executors for failing to take this precaution. Therefore, a valid method to be used by the executors.

Where a property sale needs completing or such like the procedure for a grant ad colligenda bona is simple and quick being commonly made to the registrar and can be made without notice based on an affidavit.

---

10 I have issued one of these applications instead of making a removal of executor of application due to an executor deliberately refusing to sell the Deceased's family home. Having gone through the process I would be tempted just to go straight for removal of executor proceedings as typically even if you succeed you are left with the problem of an executor who still has to distribute the assets.

Procedure

Application for the grant must include a supporting affidavit in which the grounds for the application must be stated (NCPR r. 52). Unless the application is likely to be contentious it may be made without notice (see Ghafoor).

Post-Grant

An executor/personal representative (PR) has a duty to account to the court. References: Re Tillot [1892] 1 Ch 86 A residuary beneficiary is entitled to request estate accounts from the PR detailing the composition of the estate and its liabilities.

Once requested, these should be prepared within a reasonable period (Re Tillot). This right also applies to creditors.

If probate has been obtained these are the following options to bring the executor to account.

Inventory and account - The Now Very Unpredictable Application

In the past my favourite application as it can achieve so much and with respect to executors who are committing fraud, it can provide access to bank accounts which fraudulent executors hate; it is also inexpensive. I have seen the most obstructive executors fold once they have faced a costs order and the threat of committal if they breach an order.

In the past the advantage it is the quickest way to compel a lazy or uncommunicative executor to account for his activities is to apply for an order that he exhibit an inventory and account in respect of the administration (see AEA s.25(b)).

However the appeal of an inventory and account is tempered by the erratic nature of Probate Registries and the fact that delays seem inevitable. As a consequence I am not such a fan and currently use is on simple Estates which are relatively low in value.

Procedure

Send a 14-day warning letter (please do not neglect this and jump in).

The summons form is under review[11]; otherwise prepare a Summons which is sent to the High Court together with a supporting affidavit or witness statement (NCPR r. 61).

The Court will send back the sealed summons which you will send to the Respondent and you will need to produce evidence of service. The beneficiaries of an estate are entitled to request the personal representative to provide an inventory and account. This longstanding right is now contained in s. 25 of the Administration of Estates Act 1925.

In order to get up to speed a very useful case and easy to read judgment is in the case of Ali v Taj.[12]

This case is an excellent starting point for understanding inventory and account and restates some points at paragraph 55.

One of the increasing trends of inventory and account applications is the ability to make paper (Directions Rule 61(5) of the NCPR 1987.) where the Court will make an order without arranging a hearing. This can save cost and there is still the potential to claim costs. In this scenario you can submit your statement of costs at the same time as submitting your application.

---

11 Currently consider locating a form with the issue of summons: Tristram and Coote's Probate Practice [25.236].

12 Taj v Ali [2020] EWHC 213 Fam

If the Respondent ignores an Inventory and Account, you can apply to obtain a Penal Notice. This is a notice endorsed on an order, providing that a defendant may be found to be guilty of contempt of court if the defendant fails to comply with the terms of the order. A penal notice is a warning to the defendant that disobedience to the order may be punishable by imprisonment, a fine, confiscation of assets or other punishment under the law (CPR 81.2).

Do not get sucked into massive costs on enforcing penal notices. If an executor ignores a penal notice the hassle and of cost of enforcing is not worth it. Just get on and start removal of executor proceedings.[13]

The Appeal of CPR PART 64

1. If the financial issues are complex. Sometimes the blunt tool of inventory and account is limited. In this case you should commence Part 64 legal proceedings [14]within the High Court as a mechanism. The downside is you face greater costs risks but on a matters of complexity Part 64 is the way to go to.

2. On matters of financial complexity you should also consider instructing a forensic accountant to give added strength to your arguments.

---

13 If you are still minded to make a penal notice I refer you to the Civil Procedure Rules Part 81. Your client must seek permission from the Court before making a committal application. The application notice must be supported by an affidavit. You should file an Committal application together with a Part 8 Claim form with a supporting affidavit (see Civil Procedure Rules Part 81.14) The Court fee to issue the Claim form is £528.00, as it must be issued in the High Court. You will also have to pay the application fee of £255.00.

14 https://www.justice.gov.uk/courts/procedure-rules/civil/rules/part64

The Court has wide power under CPR Part 64 to direct such accounts and inquiries as necessary. Where the action is for an account it can be brought under this part and is supported by a Claim form. We cover this form of application later and increasingly I prefer this as an option.

Judicial trustee

It is also still possible for a beneficiary to apply to the court under s.1 of the Judicial Trustees Act 1896 (JTA) for the appointment by the court of a judicial trustee to administer the estate either together with the current executor, or as a replacement.

The judicial trustee is entitled to remuneration out of the estate by order of the court.

It is widely recognised that in the clear majority of cases the appointment of a judicial trustee is an unnecessarily expensive and drawn out process, and a s.50 application to replace or remove an executor will be far preferable.

Since 1985 it is no longer necessary to appoint a Judicial Trustee to continue the administration of an estate.

Thus, the Judicial Trustee Act 1896 has largely fallen into disuse. However, the Official Solicitor often prefers to be appointed as a Judicial Trustee, so as to be able to make informal applications to the court for directions (see Judicial Trustee Rules 1983 r8).

Furthermore, the powers of a Judicial Trustee are wider than a personal representative, so where the estate is complicated, a Judicial Trustee may be a better choice (see Re Ridsdel [1947] Ch 597)

The application can be useful in these circumstances:

An application for a judicial trustee may be more sensible than a s.50 application is in the context of mutual wills (see Thomas and Agnes Carvel Foundation v Carvel [2007] 4 All ER 81).

Where the administration of an estate is likely to be particularly complicated for some reason. In this case, the appointment of a judicial trustee may be considered since they would have easier access to guidance and supervision from the court and can seek directions at any time. This can be more practical for all concerned but may also act as a safeguard for the beneficiaries.

Administration proceedings

Finally, the beneficiaries can make administration proceedings – Administration orders are now unusual. This is reflected in the fact that under CPR PD64 paragraph 3.1 the court will only make an administration order if it considers that the issues between the parties cannot properly be resolved in any other way. Please consider CPR PD 64.

RENUNCIATION FORM

IN THE HIGH COURT OF JUSTICE FAMILY DIVISION THE [PRINCIPAL (or) (name) DISTRICT PROBATE] REGISTRY

In the Estate of (name) deceased WHEREAS (full true name of deceased) of (full permanent private address) deceased, died on the (date) having made and duly executed (his/her) last will and testament dated (date) [with a codicil dated (date)] and in the [will (or) codicil] appointed (names of executors) as executors [and residuary legatees and devisees in trust]. Now I (name of executor) being one of the executors do declare that I have not intermeddled in the estate of the deceased, and will not hereafter intermeddle in the estate with intention to defraud creditors, and I do now renounce all my right and title to probate and execution of the will [and codicil] [and to letters of administration (with the will annexed) of the estate of the deceased]

DATED this

day of

20

SIGNED by

(name of executor) in the presence, of

Witness Signature:

.... Witness Name:

.... Witness Address:

....

.... Witness Occupation:

CHAPTER FIVE

REMOVAL OF EXECUTORS

> **TIP**
>
> If you have a situation where you are involved in an elderly fraud case and the person whom you suspect has committed elderly fraud is an executor and the Deceased has died it must follow that you will consider a removal of executor claim. If you end up issuing the case in the High Court Business and Property Courts you have the potential to have your claim heard promptly. Due to the efficiency of E-Filing a removal of executor is a very appealing Court forum to be heard but there are a number of variables to consider before embarking on this course of action. After all, it is such a draconian step to be taken.

Variables

1. Time can be an important variable but if elderly fraud has taken place this can justify early action. Has one year elapsed since the Deceased died and is the Executor justified in delaying distribution?

2. Do you have any specific indication of fraud from the Executor and how have you presented such evidence?

3. Has the Executor ignored any previous Court orders and correspondence from you. To what extent have you complied with the CPR?

4. Do you need the Executor to be replaced to ensure that the estate will be distributed?

5. Are there reasons why your proposed replacement executor is not suitable?

6. Are there any weaknesses in your client's case and can they be mitigated?

TIP

We cover this below but at time of writing the defining law for a removal of executor case (assuming you are making a Section 50 application) is the Earwicker case and the passage of Chief Justice Marsh and Paragraph 9.[15] We reference that brief passage below but it is critical that you have an understanding of that passage. It is so influential in how you conduct a removal of executor case.

What is an executor of a will?

When somebody dies, the executor named in their will ultimately has to ensure that the deceased's estate is properly wound up and their wishes in their will are carried out. There are many legal responsibilities associated with being an executor, including potentially:

- registering the death
- arranging the funeral
- valuing the estate
- paying any inheritance tax

[15] [2015] EWHC 1915 (CH), 2015 WL 4275082

- applying for probate
- sorting the deceased's finances
- placing a deceased estates notice
- distributing the estate
- keeping estate accounts

With cases of these kinds, it is really worth stepping back and establishing if the executor can be removed. It is very easy to get sucked into the emotion of the situation and form judgments either against or for the complaining party.

Generally, this type of application is used to remove a personal representative where the Grant of Probate has already been taken.

However, in Goodman v Goodman [2013] EWHC 758 (Ch), the High Court held that the court's powers under s50 of the Administration of Justice Act 1985 can be exercised before a Grant of Probate has been obtained.

Do you want to use Section 50 of the Administration of Justice Act 1985 to remove the Executor?

Renounce?

We cover this elsewhere, but you can explore getting the Executor to renounce (provided intermeddling has not taken place).

Citation?

Where named executors refuse to take steps to obtain a Grant but will also not renounce their rights, it is possible to force their hand by using the citation process.

Section 116(1) of the Senior Courts Act 1981? (SCA 1981)?

This can apply pre a grant of probate being obtained but I rarely use this.

The law provides that: 'If by reason of any special circumstances it appears to the High Court to be necessary or expedient to appoint as administrator some person other than the person who, but for this section, would in accordance with the probate rules have been entitled to the grant, the court may in its discretion appoint as administrator such person as it thinks expedient.'

Here, the court has the power to pass over an executor even if they have intermeddled in the estate. An executor who can no longer renounce their appointment but wishes to be passed over in favour of another may therefore have recourse to an application under SCA 1981, s 116.

The Non-Contentious Probate Rules 1987, SI 1987/2024, r 52 states that an application for an order under SCA 1981, s 116: '…may be made to a [district judge or] registrar and shall be supported by an affidavit [or witness statement] setting out the grounds of the application.'

An order can therefore be made by a district judge of the Principal Registry or a registrar of a district probate registry.

The application is usually made without notice to the registrar at the registry at which the application for a grant is being made. The registrar may then give directions, e.g. for the application to be made by summons on notice and served on interested parties.

As the application will (initially, at least) be without notice, the affidavit or witness statement should provide full information and disclosure of every fact known to the applicant that may be relevant to the court's decision.

Section 41 of the Trustee Act 1925?

If none of these provisions gives the dissatisfied beneficiary a remedy one can consider s41 of the Trustee Act 1925, where the court may make an order appointing a new trustee or new trustees either in substitution for or in addition to any existing trustee or trustees. Trustee includes personal representative for this purpose.

TIP

Consider making an Open Offer.

On a removal of executor case a tactic I sometimes use is to make an open offer to the other side e.g. I provide three names of professional executors, give the Defendant(s) of choice and say that you will not seek costs against them (e.g. out of the Estate). This may make your client look more reasonable before the Judge.

The Law of Section 50 of the Administration of Justice Act 1985

Generally, the go-to-legislation is that of Section 50 of the Administration of Justice Act 1985 which states:

Power of High Court to appoint substitute for, or to remove, personal representative.

> *(1) Where an application relating to the estate of a deceased person is made to the High Court under this subsection by or on behalf of a*

personal representative of the deceased or a beneficiary of the estate, the court may in its discretion—

(a) appoint a person (in this section called a substituted personal representative) to act as personal representative of the deceased in place of the existing personal representative or representatives of the deceased or any of them; or

(b) if there are two or more existing personal representatives of the deceased, terminate the appointment of one or more, but not all, of those persons.

(2) Where the court appoints a person to act as a substituted personal representative of a deceased person, then—

(a) if that person is appointed to act with an executor or executors the appointment shall (except for the purpose of including him in any chain of representation) constitute him executor of the deceased as from the date of the appointment; and

(b) in any other case the appointment shall constitute that person administrator of the deceased's estate as from the date of the appointment.

(3) The court may authorise a person appointed as a substituted personal representative to charge remuneration for his services as such, on such terms (whether or not involving the submission of bills of charges for taxation by the court) as the court may think fit.

(4) Where an application relating to the estate of a deceased person is made to the court under subsection (1), the court may if it thinks fit, proceed as if the application were, or included, an application for the appointment under the Judicial Trustees Act 1896 of a judicial trustee in relation to that estate.

(5) In this section "beneficiary", in relation to the estate of a deceased person, means a person who under the will of the deceased or under the law relating to intestacy is beneficially interested in the estate.

Thus, this legislation enables the High Court to do the following:

- Appoint a new executor in place of an existing executor.

- Appoint a new administrator in place of an existing administrator.

- Appoint a new administrator in place of all existing personal representatives.

- Terminate the appointment of a personal representative without replacing them, provided that this leaves at least one existing personal representative in place.

Whether a section 50 application will succeed is a matter for the discretion of the court and that the overriding considerations are broadly the proper administration of the estate and the welfare of the beneficiaries.

The statute itself provides no guidance as to the test to be applied by the court when exercising its discretion. There is a case law on the issue. Nonetheless, given the very fact specific nature of these sorts of disputes, the outcome of an application can be difficult dependent on the lawyer to think through the evidence and plot a course of success.

It is not necessary to establish wrongdoing or fault on the part of the executor. The court will generally replace an executor where, for example, relations between him and the beneficiaries have simply broken down to such an extent that it is no longer possible to progress the administration of the estate properly.

TIP

By far the most important case within the removal of executor forum is the Harris v. Earwicker [2015] EWHC 1915 (Ch):

- A critical summary of principles by Chief Master Marsh at paragraph 9.
- Court refused to remove executors because: the estate was largely wound up.
- Inefficient at this late stage to appoint a new firm of solicitors
- The Deceased's choice of beneficiaries carried great weight: he had thought carefully about who should act, having anticipated that their role would.
- No evidence to prove the ability of proposed replacement PRs, who were not professionals.

Here is the key wording of the passage from : Anthony John Harris, Peter Dixon Clegg, John Robin Mason v Mary Patricia Earwicker, Nicholas Paul Le Feuvre, Benjamin Charles Earwicker, Debra Joan Blake, Julie Ann Scurry:[16]

> *i. It is unnecessary for the court to find wrongdoing or fault on the part of the personal representatives. The guiding principle is whether the administration of the estate is being carried out properly. Put another way, when looking at the welfare of the beneficiaries, is it in their best interests to replace one or more of the personal representatives?*

16 [2015] EWHC 1915 (CH), 2015 WL 4275082

ii. If there is wrongdoing or fault and it is material such as to endanger the estate the court is very likely to exercise its powers under section 50. If, however, there may be some proper criticism of the personal representatives, but it is minor and will not affect the administration of the estate or its assets, it may well not be necessary to exercise the power.

iii. The wishes of the testator, as reflected in the will, concerning the identity of the personal representatives is a factor to take into account.

iv. The wishes of the beneficiaries may also be relevant. I would add, however, that the beneficiaries, or some of them, have no right to demand replacement and the court has to make a balanced judgment taking a broad view about what is in the interests of the beneficiaries as a whole. This is particularly important where, as here, there are competing points of view.

v. The court needs to consider whether, in the absence of significant wrongdoing or fault, it has become impossible or difficult for the personal representatives to complete the administration of the estate or administer the will trusts. The court must review what has been done to administer the estate and what remains to be done. A breakdown of the relationship between some or all of the beneficiaries and the personal representatives will not without more justify their replacement. If, however, the breakdown of relations makes the task of the personal representatives difficult or impossible, replacement may be the only option.

vi. The additional cost of replacing some or all of the personal representatives, particularly where it is proposed to appoint professional persons, is a material consideration. The size of estate and the scope and cost of the work which will be needed will have to be considered.

TIP

A successful removal of executor application entails months of planning and execution unless you have cast iron evidence of fraud (have you considered instructing a forensic accountant?) and essentially once you have a paper trail of correspondence you should be good to go. Remember the key aspect of this kind of application is the need to frontload the work. Essentially your goal is to create a compelling case within the proceedings to remove the executor. If you cannot do this within the original claim form and supporting statement you are wasting your time.

In the case of Goodman v Goodman [2013] All ER 118 which involved an appeal against a decision to remove an executor under s.50 Administration of Justice Act 1985 the rationale for the appeal was that the incorrect procedure had been used by the claimants. As this was an application to remove an executor before the grant had been obtained, it was argued that the procedure under s.116 Senior Courts Act 1981 should have been used. The appeal failed.

Historically, in cases of actual wrongdoing or fraud (such as in Alkin v Raymond) the courts were reluctant to remove personal representatives. The overriding principle remains that the court will only remove an executor if it is in the interest of the proper administration of the estate and would promote the welfare of the beneficiaries, which will depend upon the peculiar facts of each case.

In the case of Riley v. Seed [2013] EWHC 4863 (Ch) friction and hostility justified removal where it had resulted in an impasse and notwithstanding that deceased had chosen executors the best way to break the impasse was to appoint an independent professional executor.

In Nwosu v. Nwosu [2018] EWHC 1529 (Ch) the court was satisfied that there was a sufficient breakdown of trust that directly impeded the administration of the estate that executors should be replaced by professional PR as 5 years since probate granted, estate consisted of properties which need to be sold but had not been.

The case Lane v Lane 2024 EWHC 275 (Ch) - There is some very useful analysis on removal of executors in the recent case of Lane v Lane (2024 EWHC 275 (Ch)) paragraphs 60 to 63. (Judge, Jonathan Hilliard KC sitting as Deputy Judge of the High Court). This provides useful information on the law. In this case the Judge picked up on the failure to provide Estate Accounts by the Executor (see paragraph 89).

Conflict of Interest and Lifetime Transactions

This can be a key issue in elderly fraud cases.

In re Folkes decd, Griffin v. Higgs [2017] EWHC 2559 (Ch) the executors were removed because a number of lifetime transfers made by deceased, at a time when she was suffering dementia, and with the assistance of the executors, required investigation. The resulting conflict of interest meant that the executors could not conduct the investigations themselves.

The appropriate test to be applied to each allegation was "whether there appears to be on the evidence before the court, or with such evidence that appears likely to be obtained at proportionate cost, the basis for a claim which has reasonable prospects of success, subject to consideration of potential defences. Such a claim must enhance the value of the estate relative to the costs of pursuing it." (para 41)

The Deceased made a will before disputed lifetime transfers and so did not take them into consideration when choosing her executors; thus, her choice of executors, whilst a factor, could be disregarded.

Other factors in support of the removal were: majority of beneficiaries supported removal; the costs of replacement were warranted; the inevitable duplication from three professional executors would be reduced by a single replacement.

Procedure

If a s.50 application is not being made in the course of existing proceedings, it should be brought in the Chancery Division of the High Court using a Part 8 Claim Form and supported by written evidence (see CPR Part 57).

If there is more than one executor, the others must all be joined as parties, often together with the residuary beneficiaries. If a sole executor is being removed, a substitute should be sought otherwise the estate will be left unrepresented.

Applications under section 50 are governed by the Civil Procedure Rules r.57.13 and PD57, paragraphs 12–14: and must be brought in the High Court.

All applications will be assigned to the Chancery Division.

Every personal representative of the estate shall be joined as a party.

The Court Fee is £626 within the High Court. To issue a claim for something other than money the fees are based on where you start your claim e.g. Part 8 claim and civil injunctions – fees order 1.5 and 1.8: High Court (including possession claims).

Under a part 8 Claim Form -

The application must be supported by the following:

- A certified sealed copy of the Grant of Probate or Letters of Administration.

- A witness statement setting out the reasons why the removal or substitution of the Executor is sought (referring to his disqualification)

- A witness statement of the proposed substitute's executor's capacity to act[17]

- Draft order

WHAT SHOULD THE WITNESS STATEMENT INCLUDE?

It should exhibit the will and probate of the Deceased. This is the critical document which will make or break your case. It needs to be both comprehensive and succinct and consist of a compelling case of why the Executor should be removed and the suitability of the proposed replacement executor. A draft statement is provided with Appendix 1.

Once you have your claim issued it should move along to having some form of Directions appointment before a Master. You will have two issues to consider. Preparation of the Court Bundle and a Skeleton Argument. If you do a Skeleton Argument, ensure that it is succinct and no more than five pages. Pay a lot of attention to the Trial Bundle. Do you have a set of correspondence which supports your client's case? I believe you should pay more attention to the documents within the bundle compared to a Skeleton Argument.

---

17 Rule 13.2 of PRACTICE DIRECTION 57 - https://www.justice.gov.uk/courts/procedure-rules/civil/rules/part57/pd_part57#IDAJPG2

Costs

Applications to remove or replace PRs are subject to the same regime as to costs as other civil litigation in England and Wales.

CPR 44.2 provides:

> '(1) The court has discretion as to—
>
> (a) whether the costs are payable by one party to another;
>
> (b) the amount of those costs; and
>
> (c) when they are to be paid.'

Although the court has complete discretion, applications are also subject to the same general rule, as also set out at CPR 44.2:

> '(2) If the court decides to make an order about costs—
>
> (a) the general rule is that the unsuccessful party will be ordered to pay the costs of the successful party…'

Costs in cases involving PRs (and trustees) are slightly more complex than other cases, however, given that such persons are bringing or defending claims in relation to, or on behalf of, the estate or trust fund.

If the conduct of an Executor(s) is so poor consider applying for indemnity costs.

On behalf of the Claimant
First Statement of XX
One Exhibit marked XX
Date Signed M

IN THE HIGH COURT OF JUSTICE **Claim No**

BUSINESS AND PROPERTY COURTS OF ENGLAND AND WALES

PROPERTY, TRUSTS AND PROBATE LIST (ChD)

IN THE MATTER OF THE ESTATE OF YYY
BETWEEN

MR WWW

Claimant

And

MS Z Z

Defendant

STATEMENT OF MR WWW

I WWW, of 2PX do say as follows:

1. I am the Claimant and the residuary beneficiary of the estate of W "The Deceased" who died while resident in England and Wales on 27th November 2023.

2. This witness statement is made in support of an application under Section 50 of Administration of Justice Act 1985 for amongst other things the removal of the executor, Ms ZZ as the sole executor of the Deceased and her replacement by my wife, R who I believe is best placed to be an executor due to problems with my health(I have a terminal medical condition) and the fact that my wife is fully aware of my personal affairs and she is capable of administering the estate.

3. I have provided at pages of 7 to 11 inclusive of the numbered bundles of pages exhibited to this statement and marked WWW one copy of the Will and grant of Probate issued on 29th July 2019 out of N District Probate Registry.

4. The reasons for the application are as follows.

5. The Deceased made a will dated 20th June 20 appointing the Defendant and me as a residuary beneficiary, with the Defendant acting as sole executor and Trustee. After the Deceased died, the Defendant instructed the law firm, L Solicitors who had prepared the Deceased's will and afterwards helped the Defendant obtain probate on 29th May which stated the probate had a gross value of £

6. Since obtaining probate the Defendant has done little else to progress the estate including failing to try to sell the house of the Deceased which she lives in, which is believed to be the main asset of the Deceased. Moreover, I have not received any money from my inheritance nor any form of update from the Defendant. I have only found what has been going on by contacting L Solicitors who due to the inaction of the Defendant have been limited in what they can say and do. I only found out

the date that probate has been obtained and value of the estate by doing an online search myself.

7. Given this impasse and the fact that it was more than one year since the Deceased died, on 13th March 20 I instructed my solicitors, FF to write to the Defendant, copying BL Solicitors in and setting my concerns over the fact that I had not received any inheritance and any news about the progress of the estate. Also, my instructing solicitors, FF, warned that if we did not receive an interim estate account within 14 days, my firm would make an application for inventory and account.

8. As a result of the lack of response, I have made an application for an inventory and account of the Deceased's estate within the N Probate Registry. In addition, my solicitors wrote on 3r to Ms Z informing her of this but heard nothing. I am still waiting to hear further from this Court to hear more about the status of my application.

9. On 21st May 20 my solicitors again wrote to the Defendant sending a Letter Before Action warning Ms Z that I was going to make an application for her removal as executor and setting out these reasons for doing so. The reasons included:

   i) Her failure to distribute the estate within 12 months of the Deceased passing away.

   ii) The fact she remained in the sole property of the Deceased, GGG with no apparent intention of moving out.

   iii) She had ignored our request for inventory and account and not provided the financial information as requested.

   iv) The fact I had concerns the gross value of the estate may be undervalued.

10. As a result of the above, I believe it is the interests of justice that the Defendant should be removed as executor and I request the Court grant me the relief sought in the form of the attached order.

STATEMENT OF TRUTH I believe that the facts stated in this witness statement are true. I understand that proceedings for contempt of court may be brought against anyone who makes or causes to be made, a false statement in a document verified by a statement of truth without an honest belief in its truth.

Signed ....

Dated ....

CHAPTER SIX

WILL VALIDITY AND FRAUD

On a potential will fraud case you should take a step back and just go through the formalities and to assess has the will been done correctly.

As a general observation if you are facing a will prepared by solicitors it is going to be difficult to allege specific will fraud unless you have exceptional evidence.

Where you are more likely to allege fraud is wills without professional advice. Thus the focus of your approach is on the will formalities process, witnesses, background evidence and any expert evidence.

If you do use handwritten expert evidence make sure you do your due diligence on your expert evidence. You also need to be very mindful of the possible legal costs involved as these can really increase in value and one can lose control.

Assessing the Validity of the Will & the Practice

What are the proper formalities of the will?

Age

As a general rule, a testator must have reached the age of 18 at the time of making a Will (the Wills Act 1837, s.7).

Formalities

In addition, for deaths arising after 1 January 1983, Section 9 of the Wills Act 1837 (as substituted by the Administration of Justice Act 1982, s. 17) ('the Act') says that no Will is valid unless:

- It is in writing, and signed by the Testator, or by some other person in his presence and by his direction; and
- It appears that the Testator intended by his signature to give effect to the Will; and
- The signature is made or acknowledged by the Testator in the presence of two or more witnesses present at the same time; and
- Each witness either:
  - attests and signs the Will.
  - or acknowledges his signature, in the presence of the Testator (but not normally in the presence of any other witnesses), but no form of attestation shall be necessary.

In the event these formalities are not complied with the will reverts to intestacy.

Attestation clauses

Whilst an attestation clause is not strictly required, where a will includes such a clause and, on the face of it, has been validly executed, the strongest evidence is required to show that it was not validly executed (see Sherrington v Sherrington [2005] EWCA Civ 326, [2005] WTLR 587 at [40-41] and Royal National Institute for Deaf People and others v Turner [2015] EWHC 3301).

The burden of proof is on the person propounding the will, insofar as these are inconsistent with Sherrington, these are not binding on a Court.

What Is Intestacy?

In the event that the will is invalid you will either be left with the previous will or the rules of intestacy will apply.

What are the rules of intestacy?

When a person dies without leaving a valid will, their property (the estate) must be shared out according to certain rules. These are called the rules of intestacy. A person who dies without leaving a will is called an intestate person. Please see Appendix 1 for more details of intestacy. Also consider government rules: https://www.gov.uk/inherits-someone-dies-without-will

What is the form of the signature?

The signature of the testator can be merely a mark (for example a thumb prints as in Borman v Lel).[18]

Can Someone Below 18 Make a Valid Will?

Not unless they have privileged access.

Section 11 of the WA states the formal requirements do not apply to:

[18] Borman v Lel [2001] 6 WLUK 189,

Any soldier being in actual military service, or any mariner or seaman at sea… though under the age of eighteen years.

Where Does the Will Have to Be Signed?

It does not have to be "at the foot or end thereof" (following the AJA 1982 s 17).

It can be signed by someone other than the testator as it or her direction.

Who Can Prepare a Will?

Anyone can prepare a will.

Nevertheless, suspicion will be raised if the person who prepares it is:

- A major beneficiary
- A close relative of a major beneficiary
- A partner of a major beneficiary

There is no rule that prohibits one of the above preparing the will, but suspicions will be raised.

What Mental Capacity Do You Have to Have to Make a Will?

The common law standard was laid down in Banks v Goodfellow and remains the leading case which is that the testator must:

a) Understand the nature of his act (sound mind) that is he is making a will and its effects?

b) Understand the extent of his property being disposed of (sound memory) though he/she does not need remember every one of his assets.

c) Be able to comprehend and appreciate the claims to which a person making a will ought to give effect (sound understanding).

What Is the Burden of Proof?

The common law rules regarding burden of proof concerning testamentary capacity are set out in Key v Key (2010):

a) While the burden starts with the propounder of a will to establish capacity, where the will is duly executed and appears rational on its face then the court will presume capacity.

b) In such a case the evidential burden then shifts to the objector to raise a real doubt about capacity.

c) If a real doubt is raised, the evidential burden shifts back to the propounder to establish capacity, nevertheless.

Provided the testator had testamentary capacity at the time the will was signed and witnessed it may not matter if the testator loses full capacity. Generally, the time to test whether capacity existed is the time of execution of the will. However, the dates and still valid case of Parker v Felgate confirms that, in limited and defined circumstances, a Will can still be valid, even if the testator loses capacity between giving instructions and signing the Will. As long as T had capacity when giving instructions, Parker v Felgate confirms that a much lower degree of understanding is necessary when the Will is signed.

Knowledge and Approval

The testator must know and approve the contents of the will (this is not applicable to a statutory will).

The legal test is that the testator must know and approve the contents of the will at the time of execution.

In all cases, however, and irrespective of age, it is necessary to provide clients with proper advice and to assess whether it is necessary to obtain medical evidence.

Further, a client should be advised that, in the event of a subsequent challenge to their will on the basis of lack of capacity, a lack of contemporaneous medical opinion may make the challenge more likely to succeed.

Case: Brennan – v – Prior 2013 EWHC 287(ch)

The case of Brennan v Prior provides a useful illustration of how the Courts assess claims that a testator lacked knowledge of, or did not approve, the contents of his or her Will.

To admit a Will to proof, the court must be satisfied that the testator understood what he was doing and its effect so that the document represents his testamentary intentions. It is for the party seeking to propound the Will to show that the testator understood his Will.

Where a Will was executed in accordance with the formalities set out in section 9 of the Wills Act 1837 by a person with testamentary capacity there is usually a presumption the testator knew and approved its contents.

In addition, a "very strong" presumption exists where the Will was prepared by a solicitor and read over to the testator before execution.

A party seeking to propound a Will may not be able to rely simply on due execution and capacity where the circumstances surrounding its preparation or execution "excite the suspicion of the Court" – where the Will was drafted by a person who benefits under it or contains complex provisions which the testator was unlikely to understand.

A party seeking successfully to challenge a Will must produce evidence of circumstances which leaves the Court not satisfied that, on the balance of probabilities, the testator understood its nature and effect, and sanctioned the dispositions it made.

Given this it is critical that the lawyer is satisfied that there is strong evidence to show an absence of knowledge and approval from the testator.[19]

Presumption of Due Execution

In the case of Channon v Perkins[20] it was said that where the will had a full and valid attestation clause and represented the deceased's wishes, there must be cogent and clear evidence, i.e., testimony which constitutes 'the strongest evidence', to overturn a will.

Recently there has been two significant cases which challenged the validity of wills on the basis of a lack of testamentary capacity.

Here we will look at the cases.

---

19 Some useful summaries of the law - https://www.thegazette.co.uk/all-notices/content/103463

Baker & Anor v Hewston [2023] EWHC 1145 (Ch)

The case of Baker & Anor v Hewston raised the question of whether the test for testamentary capacity should remain the Banks v Goodfellow test or whether the Mental Capacity Act 2005 (MCA) should replace it.

This question has been repeatedly asked and considered in case law since the MCA came into force.

The MCA (ss.2-3) sets out alternate criteria for testamentary capacity:

1. Assess whether the person has an impairment of their mind or brain, preventing the person from making a decision in relation to the matter, regardless of age or appearance.

2. A person is unable to make a decision for themselves if they are unable to:

    - understand the information relevant to the decision

    - retain that information

    - use or weigh that information as part of the process of making the decision

    - communicate his/her decision

The *Baker v Hewston* judgment suggested that both tests could and should be used concurrently; the MCA to act as a cross-check to *Banks v Goodfellow.* If the MCA test suggested a different result, this should lead to further consideration of the testator's capacity.

In 2017 the Law Commission had recommended that the *Banks v Goodfellow* test be replaced by the test under the MCA, or alternatively put on a statutory footing, but this has yet to be considered by parliament.

Leonard v Leonard [2024] EWHC 321 (Ch)

This case firmly reinforces that the *Banks v Goodfellow* test very much remains good law, having '*stood the test of time*'.

The judgment examined the four limbs of the test in some detail and set out an authoritative and comprehensive summary of how the courts should approach them, noting developments in modern medical understanding regarding capacity issues.

In *Leonard v Leonard*, the will was prepared by a chartered tax advisor employed in a law firm, but her evidence was strongly criticised as showing no awareness of capacity issues.

The judgment endorsed the view expressed in *Re Ashkettle 2013* that *"[a]ny view the solicitor may have formed as to the testator's capacity must be shown to be based on a proper assessment and accurate information or it is worthless".*

Summary

The commentary on *Leonard v Leonard* suggests that going forward this case will be considered the leading authority on testamentary capacity cases.

However, one should observe the judgment raised is a warning to proceed with caution:

> *"Parties to cases of this sort should be under no illusions as to the emotional and financial toll the extract and the considerable ordeal for both sides of contesting the matter to a final judgment."*

Practical Steps

- If the attesting witnesses are available, try to take witness statements from them separately (from each other, if possible), and do so early where evidence may be relatively fresh in mind.

- Obtain handwriting evidence in the right cases – but instruct the right expert, be mindful of its limitations, and consider carefully what the scope of the instruction should be (i.e. is it the signature only, or a broader enquiry?)

- Be realistic with time estimates. Forgery claims will usually involve cross-examination of at least one, likely three, and possibly more witnesses who are playing with the facts. Unpicking that takes time.

- Be careful how you make allegations.

What is Will Forgery?

Forging a testamentary document (such as a Will or letter of Wishes) can have serious consequences, as was witnessed in the recent case of Stewart Pearman, 75, who was sentenced to over 5 years in prison for forging a letter to solicitors fraudulently staking his claim to the £2 million estate of an elderly friend.[21]

Mr Pearman, an acquaintance of 25 years to the deceased and an executor to her Will, prepared a 'letter of wishes' placing himself as the main beneficiary of the Will, which had previously pledged to leave the multimillion-pound fortune to an air ambulance charity instead of himself.

---

21 https://www.bbc.co.uk/news/uk-england-gloucestershire-64511847

After the testator died on August 7th, 2016, Pearman presented the letter to solicitors, who became suspicious and began an investigation.

Will forgery is a criminal offence under sections 1 – 4 of the Forgery and Counterfeiting Act 1981 and could result in a maximum of 10 years imprisonment.

In criminal proceedings, the standard of proof is greater; the court must be convinced beyond reasonable doubt that forgery occurred. This increased burden reflects the more serious implications of a criminal conviction.

The ultimate responsibility of showing that a Will is not a forgery must be on the party seeking to advance the Will.

A useful case to consider is that of Watts v Watts.[22]

In this case Master Clark handed down judgment in a case concerning an allegedly forged will.

The Claimant, Carlton Watts, had brought proceedings against his mother, Jobyna Watts, for allegedly forging her late husband's will ("the Will"). Mr Watts alleged Ms Watts had used the will of his brother, Fraser Watts – produced and witnessed by the attesting solicitor two weeks apart – as a template from which to forge the Will.

The case highlights the importance placed on the evidence of an attesting witness and, in addition, the extent to which an expert's opinion withstands scrutiny in cross examination. Master Clark concluded the Will was not a forgery.

An instance of a forgery exposed was when the Telegraph reported the true story of a young wife, who forged her deceased elderly husband's will

---

22 https://www.bailii.org/ew/cases/EWHC/Ch/2023/679.html

in a bid to secure the lion's share of his estate. [23] Marsha Henderson married retired London bus conductor turned school patrolman, Newton Davies, in 2004, when she was in her twenties and he was 76. She "concocted" a fake will, which she claimed to have found hidden inside a discarded bag of Doritos crisps in the attic of her dead husband's west London home. Following his death in 2013 at the age of 85 - and after finding out he had left her just £25,000 of his of £600,000 fortune - she decided to "orchestrate a fraud" in an attempt to secure more than half-a-million pounds, it was said.

Unsurprisingly the judge picked on the fact that the most striking defect is that the attestation clause itself refers to it being "HER last will." The deceased was a man and not a woman.

The Inherent Difficulty of Forgery Claims Even With Good Handwritten Evidence

From experience there has been a reluctance to find that the testator's signature has been forged, mainly because of the seriousness of an allegation of forgery and the difficulty of proof.

In Fuller v Strum [2002] 1 WLR 1097 a joint handwriting expert found that there was very strong positive evidence of forgery. However, the trial Judge declined to make a finding of forgery, since that would have involved a conclusion that the persons present when the Will was allegedly signed had been guilty of fraud. There was no appeal from this aspect of the judgment.

In Wyniczencko v Plucinska-Surowka [2005] EWHC 2794 one expert concluded that there was very strong evidence that the testatrix's signature had been forged; the findings of the other expert were

[23] https://www.telegraph.co.uk/news/2017/05/08/woman-20s-married-lollipop-man-76-forged-will-bid-secure-600k/

inconclusive. The Judge stated that there was a real possibility of forgery, but that he was not satisfied on the balance of probabilities that the Will was forged by the sole beneficiary.

However the ultimate responsibility of showing that a Will is not a forgery must be on the party seeking to advance the Will.

In addition to expert testimony, witness evidence regarding pertinent topics will be crucial. This could include such matters as the circumstances and timing of the discovery of a Will, what the testator may have informed others about creating their Will, or the testator's Will-making history.

In circumstances involving charges of fraud (for example, if a Will's signature is legitimate but the person signing it had no idea what they were signing), the evidence of those allegedly participating in the scam will be especially relevant.

Handwriting experts and discrepancies between signatures may help tip the scales where there is suspicion of any falsification but unfortunately, even when proven guilty, there are circumstances where even the perpetrators could potentially benefit.

In Patel v Patel [2017] EWHC 133 (Ch), Andrew Simmonds QC found that a will had been forged by one of the testatrix's four sons. The claimant sought to prove a will of which he was sole executor and beneficiary, which would have given him control of a $50m stake in a family company.

Careful With Defensive Tactics

One of the possible defences which can be applied by a would beneficiary trying to prevent probate is requiring it to be proved in solemn form will benefit from costs protection (r.57.7(5)).

In determining the principle of costs, courts can and will have regard to the conduct of the parties both before and during the proceedings.

Offers of settlement, whether or not made under Part 36 of the CPR, can be taken into account. The general rule that costs follow the event may be disapplied in appropriate cases.

A recent decision of the High Court in the matter of Lumb –v- Lumb [2023] EWHC 2052 (Ch) shows the costs risks involved in Probate claims against an Estate.

In Lumb, a son (S) of the Deceased sought to challenge the validity of her Will on grounds that she lacked capacity at the time that it was made. However, S did not appear to actively progress that claim before the Courts for an extended period of time, and eventually the Estate's Executor / S's brother (M) applied to the Court to pronounce in favour of the Deceased's Will.

In his Defence, S did not seek to raise any positive case against the Estate but instead applied to cross-examine the witnesses who attested the Will at the time of its creation.

Probate claims are partly governed by Part 57 of the Civil Procedure Rules, and S sought to rely upon a specific provision within those rules (Rule 57.7) which stipulates that;

> *"a defendant may give notice in his defence that he does not raise any positive case, but insists on the will being proved in solemn form and, for that purpose, will cross-examine the witnesses who attested the will… if a defendant gives such a notice, the court will not make an order for costs against him unless it considers that there was no reasonable ground for opposing the will."*

Although S sought to rely upon this provision, and invoke the costs protection that it affords, the High Court held that S had not at any point raised an argument that could be considered reasonable grounds for opposing the Will. On appeal, the High Court awarded costs in favour of M accordingly.

In giving judgment, the High Court considered in detail the application of the usual 'costs follow the event' rule that applies to civil disputes, i.e. that the successful party in any litigation will generally be entitled to recover their costs (or a portion thereof) from the unsuccessful party.

While CPR Rule 57.7 provides a general exception to that rule, the Court highlighted that a) the inquisitorial rule of the Court in probate cases is much less than it once was and b) the Courts are increasingly concerned to avoid encouraging litigation, and discouraging settlement, by removing the usual costs follow the event rule.

In the circumstances, the Court held that there was no reasonable ground for S opposing the Will, and accordingly that M in successfully bringing the claim was also entitled to his costs.

The case illustrates the wide discretion available to the Court in connection with the issue of costs, and acts as a reminder that in probate cases of the costs risks.

Pre-Action Protocol

There is no specific protocol for validity disputes but parties in order to comply with this need to exchange as much as information as possible to allow themselves to understand the side's position as much as possible.

> **TIP**
>
> Personally I believe the ultimate approach to settling a case before the issue of legal proceedings is the well drafted letter offering settlement possibly on an open basis. However this is most likely to work if the opponent and his or her lawyer is intelligent enough to play ball. While ADR can be effective and is enshrined in the Civil Procedure Rules there is cost involved in going through the mediation process which may not be recoverable.

Make appropriate attempts to resolve the case by ADR if possible.

In addition, the Association of Contentious Trust and Probate Specialists[24] has produced its own voluntary Code for probate disputes which contains useful information and precedents and states that:

The Scope of The Code

This Code is intended to apply to "trust and probate disputes", which are disputes about:

- the devolution and administration of estates of deceased persons; and
- the devolution and administration of trust funds.

This Code is not intended to displace other protocols if in the circumstances of the case they can be seen to be more appropriate.

The main types of disputes under this Code are:

24 https://actaps.com/code-of-conduct/

- Contentious probate claims, which are challenges to the validity of a will, for example on grounds of want of capacity, want of knowledge and approval, undue influence or forgery
- Applications under the Inheritance (Provision for Family and Dependants) Act 1975 ("the Inheritance Act")
- Applications for the removal of an administrator, executor or trustee or the appointment of a judicial trustee
- Applications for the rectification of a will, trust instrument or other document
- Disputes about the meaning of provisions in a will or a trust
- Claim alleging breach of trust.

The ACTAPS Code may also apply to certain types of disputes where the provisions of a trust or the devolution of an estate are important, for example where a claimant seeks as part of their claim to set aside or overturn a trust or to take advantage of rights under a trust.

The Code has two aims:

"To encourage the resolution of disputes without hostile litigation; and

Even where litigation may be necessary, to try to simplify the litigation by exchanging relevant information before litigation has commenced."

Use the Code To get Medical Notes

As the Code says at 2.11 *In a probate dispute, medical notes may be highly relevant and it should be assumed for the purposes of the Code that they ought to be disclosed, unless there is a special reason not to disclose them.*

In an elderly fraud case medical notes are likely to be factor and you should get hold of them and/or disclose them sooner rather than later.

Issuing the Claim

The claimant prepares the claim form (Form N2) stating:

- the deceased's name
- the claimant(s) name(s)
- the defendant(s)' name(s) and address(es)
- brief details of the claim, including a statement of the nature of the interest of the claimant and of each defendant in the deceased's estate[25]
- the court fee
- whether the claim includes any issues under the Human Rights Act 1998
- setting out or attaching the particulars of claim, or stating that they are to follow[26]
- completing the statement of truth. This is either signed by the claimant, their litigation friend where the claimant is a child or a patient or the claimant's legal representative

If the claim is for the revocation of the grant, every person who is entitled or claims to be entitled to administer the deceased's estate under an

25 CPR 57.7(1)

26 CPR 7.4(1)(a)

unrevoked grant of probate of the Will or letters of administration must be made a party to the claim.[27]

How many copies of the claim form?

The claimant should prepare two copies of the claim form to file at court and further copies for service on each defendant.

The claimant takes or sends the claim form (and copies) to the issuing office at the court.

The claimant must pay the court fee to issue proceedings. It is £569 in the High Court and £332 in the County Court.

Once the claim is issued the original claim form and copies for service are returned to the claimant and the court copy is filed. The proceedings receive a claim number, which must be inserted at the top of all other forms in the proceedings.

Where the claimant is a child or protected party

If the claimant is a child or a protected party a litigation friend will need to be appointed in accordance with CPR 21.

Lodging and evidence of testamentary documents

Any testamentary document of the deceased in the claimant's possession must be lodged with the court when the claim form is issued (unless the court directs otherwise).[28]

---

27 CPR 57.6(1)

28 CPR 57.5(2)(a)

The claimant must describe any testamentary document of the deceased of which they have knowledge, or if they do not have knowledge of such testamentary document state that fact. If any testamentary document of which the claimant has knowledge is not in their possession or control, the claimant must give the name and address of the person who has possession or control of it, or if they do not know, state this fact.[29]

Once the claim is issued the court sends a notice to the Leeds District Probate Registry requesting that all testamentary documents held at any probate registry are sent to it.

Legal Proceedings

Validity disputes are brought about in the Chancery Division of the High Court CPR Practice Division 7A sets out the rules deciding whether proceedings should be commenced in the High Court or County Court.

Generally, £100,000 is the lower limit for issuing any non-personal injury case in the High Court.

Probate Claims follow the CPR Part 7 procedure but are modified in the following ways:

- The time limit for acknowledging service is 28 days after service of the particulars of claim.
- The time limit for filing the defence is also 28 days after service of the particulars of claim.

Once the action has started the relevant Court will contact Leeds District Probate Registry asking that all testamentary documents, grants of probate and any other relevant documents are sent to the relevant office.

---

29 CPR 57.5(3)

Limitation Period

There is no specific limitation period in probate claims although the defences of laches and acquiescence apply.

Other Parties

Those who are entitled under the will at issue or a previous will or on intestacy together with anyone claiming entitlement to administer the estate as Personal Representative should be joined as a party to the action.

The relevant court rules in helping to make this decision are:

CPR r 19.6 to 19.8a

The claim form should be served within 4 months of issue.

Once a case has been started under CPR 57.11 the case cannot be discontinued.

CHAPTER SEVEN

UNDUE INFLUENCE OF LIFETIME TRANSACTIONS

The law of undue Influence of lifetime transactions is easier to prove than undue influence of wills and thus can be an appealing avenue if one is alleging elderly fraud.

When an estate appears to be smaller than expected, personal representatives (PRs) and beneficiaries can have concerns about dispositions made by the deceased during their lifetime.

For example gifts, asset sales which appear to have been made at an undervalue, loans on favourable terms and solely owned assets which were transferred into joint names.

Where the deceased's affairs were being dealt with by an attorney or deputy the focus of investigations may need to include them.

TIP

As a general rule of thumb it is better to fight a case on territory which favours your client. As a consequence I would prefer to fight a case under the heading of undue influence of lifetime transactions than undue influence of a Will. Sometimes we will have no choice and/or the tactics or the facts do not work like this. It does not stop us from having a point of preference.

If I had a choice I would prefer to fight a case on undue influence of lifetime transactions than undue influence of a will.

The Background To Lifetime Transactions

In the case of Niersmans v Pesticcio [2004] EWCA Civ 372 the judge LJ Mummery identified a number of social trends that lead to pressure on the vulnerable to make life time gifts (often even their homes) of their property "*As people live longer, the inheritors will have to wait longer... the elderly and infirm in need of full time residential care are vulnerable to suggestions that they should dispose of the home to which they are unlikely to return.*"

From our experience many elderly lawyers neglect to focus on lifetime transactions as a form of scrutiny of Estates particularly at the point that probate is being obtained.

How To Pressurise Executors And/Or Beneficiaries

> **TIP**
>
> The seven years leading up to the Deceased's date of passing is a particular point of interest and on significant Estates the Executor may have to fill in the IHT 403. It can be worthwhile reminding and emphasising all parties that information provided to HMRC has to be accurate and legally compliant.

The case of *Hutchings v HMRC*[30] was an instance in which a court (the First-tier Tax Tribunal) had considered the provisions of the Finance Act 2007, Sch 24, para 1A and, whether or not HMRC were right to impose a penalty on a beneficiary who had failed to make a full and accurate disclosure to his father's executors in respect of a lifetime gift he had received from his father offshore just prior to his father's death.

---

[30] [2015] UKFTT 9 (TC)

The lifetime transfer from the Deceased to Clayton Hutchings led to an additional £47,000 of inheritance tax being due, for which Clayton Hutchings, as the recipient of the gift, was personally liable.

This is significant as it shows beneficiaries are potentially exposed, though this case is an extreme example.

HMRC also imposed a penalty of 65% of the potential loss of inheritance tax payable (£113,794) caused by the failure of Clayton Hutchings to declare the gift, although this penalty was subsequently reduced to £87,533.

HMRC have the authority to impose such a penalty under Part 1 paragraph 1(1) of Schedule 24 of the Finance Act 2007 following a failure of a recipient of a lifetime gift failing to disclose such a gift to HMRC at the relevant time.

This decision shows that as long as the executors take all reasonable steps to see the extent of any lifetime gifts and report what they are told accurately, they will not be held liable if a beneficiary misleads them or fails to disclose any such gifts (which, on the face of it, were not apparent from the records held by the executors).

Fundamentally the executors have to make all reasonable efforts when completing the IHT400 to ensure that they report properly all lifetime gifts which have become taxable to HMRC.

A beneficiary has an obligation to respond honestly and accurately to any enquiries raised with him by the executors of an estate in respect of any lifetime gifts he has received.

The case held that a beneficiary does not need to have a duty to report such gifts in order to be held liable under para 1A but in any event the recipient of a failed potentially exempt transfer does have a duty to report this to HMRC so as to report his liability to inheritance tax.

By failing to disclose the information to the executors, which in turn led to an inaccurate IHT400 being filed, the beneficiary had failed to meet his obligations and so was liable for a penalty.

What Are Some Legal Principles of Undue Influence?

> "*Persuasion is not unlawful, but pressure of whatever character if so exerted as to overpower the volition without convincing the judgment ..., will constitute undue influence, though no force has been either used or threatened*".
> Sir J P Wilde in Hall v. Hall LR 1 P&D 481, at p. 482 2.

Lifetime Transactions: mortgages, gifts, right-to-buy, contracts at undervalue etc are the usual subject matter of undue influence legal disputes.

What is the key law now?

The common law test for capacity to make a gift was set out in Re Beaney [1978] 1 WLR 770: a donor must have a high level of understanding of the fact that they are making a gift, the nature of that gift and the consequences of that gift.

The test is about ability to understand rather than actual understanding. As to the degree of understanding required: "that the mental capacity required by the law in respect of any instrument is relative to the particular transaction which is being effected by means of the instrument and may be described as the capacity to understand the nature of that transaction when it is explained."

How can transactions be set aside?

A lifetime gift can be set aside due to either actual undue influence or presumed undue influence, the manner of proof being the distinction between the two.

Lord Nicholls: Royal Bank of Scotland v. Etridge described the two forms of undue influence: a. "*Overt acts of improper pressure or coercion, such as unlawful threats*" b. "*A relationship where one has acquired over another a measure of influence or ascendancy of which the ascendant person then takes unfair advantage… without any specific acts of coercion*".

Actual v Presumed Undue Influence

The case of Royal Bank of Scotland v Etridge (No 2) [2002] 1 AC 773 showed direct proof of actual undue influence is "overt acts of improper pressure" e.g. unlawful threats and the second presumed undue influence "arises out of a relationship between two persons where one had acquired over another a measure of influence".

What is the Difference?

In the broadest possible way, the difference between the two types is that in the case of actual undue influence something has to be done to twist the mind of a donor whereas in cases of presumed undue influence it is more a case of what has not been done namely ensuring that independent advice is available to the donor.

Actual undue influence applies where there are overt acts of wrongdoing. The individual subject to the influence has been coerced or improperly pressured into doing something. For example the individual subjecting the influence may have made unlawful threats. **Generally, the burden of proving an allegation of undue influence falls to the person claiming to have been wronged.**

Presumed undue influence is for lifetime gifts where there is: a relationship of trust and confidence (such a relationship) is assumed in some incidences, namely that between parent and child, solicitor and client, medical practitioner and patient or trustee and beneficiary; and a transaction is of such a size or nature that it calls for an explanation.

At a practical level once these requirements have been satisfied, the burden of proof shifts to the person seeking to uphold the transaction to show that on the balance of probabilities the transaction was entered in to by the influenced person independently and free from influence.

If undue influence is proved then the transaction is declared void.

Legally and provided it works for you and your client presumed undue influence is the way to go as if you are successful in this area you can tactically shift the burden to the other side.

Presumed Undue Influence

One of the key legal issues is there is a presumption of undue influence for lifetime gifts where there is:

- a relationship of trust and confidence is assumed in some incidences, namely that between parent and child, solicitor and client, medical practitioner and patient or trustee and beneficiary; and

- a transaction is of such a size or nature that it calls for an explanation.

Once these requirements have been satisfied, the burden of proof shifts to the person seeking to uphold the transaction to show that on the balance of probabilities the transaction was entered in to by the influenced person independently and free from influence.

If undue influence is proved, then the transaction is declared void. A presumption of influence in certain categories of relationship, for reasons of public policy, there is a legal presumption of influence (as opposed to merely an evidential one).

A significant gift made by an elderly and/or vulnerable individual, particularly where that gift is substantial in the context of the individual's other assets is often a warning in these types of cases.

The law presumes that the person in the dominant position may have taken advantage of the other person's vulnerability or dependence (ascendancy).

The person claiming to be influenced does not need to prove the undue influence; they merely need to prove the existence of the relationship and that it was one of trust and confidence.

Presumed Undue Influence – The Importance of Ascendancy

In the case of certain relationships, namely parent and child, guardian and ward, trustee and beneficiary, solicitor and client, and medical adviser and patient, there is a legal presumption of influence (as opposed to merely an evidential one).

In Etridge (No 2), Lord Nicholls said 'in these cases the law presumes, irrebuttably, that one party had influence over the other. The complainant need not prove he actually reposed trust and confidence in the other party. It is sufficient for him to prove the existence of the type of relationship'. The existence of such relationship does not on its own create a presumption of undue influence — the second element must also be established.

Where there is no legal presumption of influence, existence of a relationship of influence must be established on the facts. A relationship of influence can be established by proof that the donor placed trust and confidence in the other party in relation to the management of the donor's financial affairs. A relationship of influence may also be proved by, for example, evidence of the donor's dependence or vulnerability. It is worth bearing in mind that closeness or mutual trust between the parties will not, by itself satisfy this element of the test, nor will the fact that the relationship imposes fiduciary duties on the alleged influencer.

The existence of a relationship of influence merely flags that it is possible that the donor was subject to undue influence when entering into a specific transaction. A presumption of undue influence will arise only if that specific transaction calls for an explanation, or if the transaction is not able to be explained on the facts.

Consider Evidence

It is important to maintain a broad overview and to look at the broad level of sums involved

Look at gifts which are substantial in the context of the donor's other liquid assets, out of proportion to the those normally shown by the donee to the donor and those which give rise to significant adverse tax implications.

Consider any explanation provided. For example, in Tociapski v Tociapski[31], the only available explanation for the transfer—that it was an estate planning measure —was rejected on the basis it was improbable.

31 [2013] EWHC 1770 (Ch)

Some Legal Examples

A legal case in respect of lifetime transactions is found in in Royal Bank of Scotland v. Etridge[32] in which it was established that if a person bringing the claim can show that there was a relationship of trust and confidence between the person alleged to have been unduly influenced and the alleged undue influencer, together with a transaction calling for an explanation, then the Claimant will have successfully discharged the burden of proof and the burden will pass to the Defendant to prove the unexplained transaction(s).

Lord Nicholl said "*A relationship where one has acquired over another a measure of influence or ascendancy of which the ascendant person then takes unfair advantage... without any specific acts of coercion.*"

In another case, Hammond v Osborne[33] a pensioner had never received independent advice in relation to the gift; The size of the gift was never brought to his attention; The pensioner did not seem to have given any consideration to his future needs and how the gift might affect this; Osborne had failed to disclose the gift to the pensioner's family and wrongly told them she had no papers relating to his estate.

Once a presumption of undue influence is raised, the burden is on person exercising influence to prove that the influenced person entered into the transaction of their own free will.

In this case the judge, Ward LJ emphasised here that in cases of presumed undue influence, the courts interfere on the grounds of public policy and not because there is any finding that there has been actual undue influence.

---

32 [2001] UKHL 44,

33 [2002] EWCA Civ 885

A gift made by an individual during their life will only be valid if made while they had sufficient mental capacity to make the decision, and while they were free from undue influence.

Litigation of such gifts will often occur after death, when estate beneficiaries or executors find that the deceased person gave away substantial assets before their death. In these situations, Court orders would be needed to overturn the gifts and claw the relevant assets back into the estate.

Capacity to make a gift is judged differently to the capacity for making a will

The test as set out in the case of Re Beaney [1978] 1 WLR 770. The standard of capacity expected is relative to the gift being made, meaning that the greater the gift – the higher the level of understanding required.

Whilst lack of capacity can lead to a gift being voidable, often there is overlap between the principles that apply to the doctrines of lack of capacity and that of undue influence, in that lower capacity can make someone more vulnerable to undue influence.

The Importance of Legal Advice With Presumed Undue Influence

Where a presumption of undue influence exists, a burden will be imposed upon the defendant to show how, in actual fact, the donor exercised a free and independent judgement without the risk of that being clouded by the donee's impact upon them.

One way in which a claim of undue influence may be defeated is by showing that the claimant received independent legal advice.

Discharging that burden by proof of the donor's receipt of independent advice.

While a donee may have capacity to make the gift it is a different question as to whether this advice freed the donee from the undue influence.[34]

If there has been competent and independent advice given to the donor then this may rebut the presumption. E.g Inche Noriah v Omar [1929] AC 127

Other Factors

In *Hewett* v. *First Plus Financial Group Plc* [2010] EWCA Civ. 312; [2010] 2 P & CR 22, the court found undue influence in a husband's failure to disclose his extramarital affair before his wife agreed to a remortgage of their property.

Similarly, and again in certain categories of relationship, the court will impose an obligation upon the influential party to take steps to bring about a form of barrier between themselves and the other person, for example by requiring that they recommend the taking of independent advice.

Failure by the influential party to take such steps has then been termed as undue influence: e.g. *Lloyds Bank* v. *Bundy* [1975] QB 326. In this case Lord Denning MR established the doctrine of an inequality of bargaining power. Here, the parties stood on unequal footing upon heading into a contractual agreement; it combines undue influence, duress, and unconscionability.

Presumed Undue Influence: Remember the Legal and Evidential Burden

The evidence required to discharge the burden of proof depends on the nature of the alleged undue influence, the personality of the parties, their

---

34 Royal Bank of Scotland plc v Etridge (No 2) [2001] UKHL 44

relationship, the extent to which the transaction cannot readily be accounted for by the ordinary motives of ordinary persons in that relationship, and all the circumstances of the case

If the term "presumed undue influence" is used it should be remembered that it is merely an example of actual undue influence but where the circumstances are that there is a shift in the evidential burden.

If the claimant proves (a) that the donor placed trust and confidence in the donee or that the donee acquired ascendancy over the donor, and (b) that the transaction calls out for explanation, the claimant has discharged an evidential burden, which will also enable an inference of undue influence to be drawn, and thus satisfy the legal burden, unless the donee produces evidence to counter the inference which would otherwise be drawn.

Property Transfer - A case of a property transfer from an elderly father to his son

It is possible that the some of the key issues you will face is on the transfer of property.

The case of Paull v Paull [2018] EWHC 2520 (Ch) involved a property transfer from an elderly father, Neville Paull, to his son, Bradey Paull.

Neville Paull lived in his property with his partner, Linda.

In 2010, when he was 67 years old and considered to be frail and vulnerable, he transferred his home to his son Bradley.

Neville argued that he only transferred the property because Bradley would look after it so he and Linda could live there for life.

Bradley stated that Neville wanted to transfer the property to ensure it did not go to Linda's children, it would not be sold to pay care home fees, and to avoid Inheritance Tax. Neville sought to have the transaction set aside on the grounds that Bradley had unduly influenced.

Neville had transferred his home to Bradley in 2010 and sought to have the transaction set outside on the grounds that he had been unduly influenced by him.

Neville was reported to be "frail and vulnerable" and submitted that he had only agreed to transfer the property to Bradley on the basis that he was allowed to remain living there (with his partner) for the rest of their lives and that Bradley would be responsible for looking after the property for him. He told the court that the transaction had been his son's idea.

Bradley said that the transaction came about so as to prevent his partner's children from different relationships benefiting after his death and to avoid the property being sold by the local authority in due course to pay care home fees. He sought to rely on the fact that his father had received legal advice from the solicitor instructed in the transaction as to the consequences of the transfer.

Master Bowles said:

> *"This is not the case of a wealthy man disposing of surplus assets, in old age, to procure fiscal, or other benefits. This is the case of an elderly man giving away the home in which he lived and which, objectively, reflected over half's assets, at a time when he was without income, other than any income derived from his other assets and where those other assets, far from being surplus were the assets upon which Neville relied to live."*

He considered the legal advice given to be insufficient and concluded ".. *this is a case where Neville entered into the transfer without the full understanding of the implications, or effects, of the transfer which is….. a necessary precondition before a court can be satisfied that the presumption of undue influence has been debuted and the presumed influence dissipated. In those circumstances, the transfer cannot stand"*.

Deathbed gifts (donatio mortis causa)

Where a person makes a gift which is not included within their Will but is intended to take effect upon death, this is referred to as a deathbed gift.

The donor must have the requisite mental capacity to make a valid lifetime gift. The further requirements for which there must be proof of compliance are that the donor:

- contemplated impending death
- made a gift which is conditional and effective on death (and until death the donor had the right to revoke the gift), and
- parted with dominion over the subject matter of the gift to the recipient

Depending on whether the asset gifted is capable of delivery, parting with dominion will involve actual delivery, constructive delivery (for example, providing a key or passcode to a safety deposit box), or delivery of the title documents, for example, title deeds.

Cases involving deathbed gifts require strict scrutiny and should be supported by 'evidence of the clearest and most unequivocal character' (*Cosnahan v Grice* (1862) 15 Moo PCC 215, 15 ER 476.

Applications to Court

> **TIP**
>
> One of the key issues you will face is how to use your allegations of unfair influence. Your client could make a specific claim under CPR part 7 or weave the argument into a Removal of Executor claim(Part 8 claim) or elsewhere. You need to think carefully about the form of legal action. Always retain an overview of your legal options. Once you start a legal process the costs will mount up and there is bound to be time spent on the legal process.

Anyone with an interest or a potential or contingent interest in the estate can make an application to the court that the PRs provide a full inventory and an account of the administration of the estate. in accordance with Administration of Estates Act 1925, s 25.

PRs should make appropriate enquiries as to any lifetime gifts made by the deceased, particularly in the seven years preceding their death.

Where there is a suggestion that a lifetime transaction may be voidable, PRs may make enquiries by, for example, obtaining medical records and contacting witnesses.

PRs who fail to take active steps when there is a suggestion that a lifetime transaction should be challenged, and allow a limitation period to expire may face a claim of devastavit (wasting of assets) for failing in their duties to collect in assets.

The PR may then be personally liable to the beneficiaries for the loss to the estate.

CHAPTER EIGHT

PART 64 PROCEEDINGS

The Downside of Inventory and Account

Currently I am not a fan of using inventory and account due to the delays and unpredictability of using the Probate Registries.

In addition, if the financial issues are complex sometimes the blunt tool of inventory and account is limited.

You can consider Part 64 legal proceedings[35] within the High Court as a way to resolve your Estate problem.

The downside is you face greater costs risks but on a matters of financial complexity Part 64 is the way to go to.

The Court has wide power under CPR Part 64 to direct such accounts and inquiries as necessary. Where the action is for an account it can be brought under this part and is supported by a Claim form.

CPR Part 64 - The Wideness of CPR Part 64

The application to claims for the determination of any question arising in the administration of an estate, or the execution of a trust is wide and will cover most claims where a trustee or beneficiary wishes the court to determine an issue that has arisen in the administration of that trust.

As a consequence this is a potential key tool for resolving fraud issues.

---

35 https://www.justice.gov.uk/courts/procedure-rules/civil/rules/part64

Generally CPR Part 64 applies to claims for the court to determine any question arising:

- in the administration of the estate of a deceased person or for the execution of a trust
- for an order for the administration of the estate of a deceased person, or for the execution of a trust, to be carried out under the directions of the court ('an administration order')
- It is also possible to seek the recovery of monies against a trustee by commencing a claim for an account.

The Range of CPR Part 64

More specifically, CPR PD 64A[36] gives examples of the types of claims which may be made under CPR 64.2(a) as follows:

> Examples of claims under rule 64.2(a)
>
> The following are examples of the types of claims which may be made under rule 64.2(a) –
>
> (1) a claim for the determination of any of the following questions –
>
> > (a) any question as to who is included in any class of persons having –
> >
> > > (i) a claim against the estate of a deceased person;

[36] https://www.justice.gov.uk/courts/procedure-rules/civil/rules/part64/pd_part64a

(ii) a beneficial interest in the estate of such a person; or

(iii) a beneficial interest in any property subject to a trust;

(b) any question as to the rights or interests of any person claiming –

(i) to be a creditor of the estate of a deceased person;

(ii) to be entitled under a will or on the intestacy of a deceased person; or

(iii) to be beneficially entitled under a trust;

(2) a claim for any of the following remedies –

(a) an order requiring a trustee –

(i) to provide and, if necessary, verify accounts;

(ii) to pay into court money which he holds in that capacity; or

(iii) to do or not to do any particular act;

(b) an order approving any sale, purchase, compromise or other transaction by a trustee (whether administrative or dispositive); or

(c) an order directing any act to be done which the court could order to be done if the estate or trust in question were being administered or executed under the direction of the court.

Part 7 or Part 8?

Where the allegations made are of dishonesty or other deliberate wrongdoing you cannot commence the claim using CPR Part 8 (as required by CPR Part 64) and so such claims should be brought under CPR Part 7.

The Part does not apply to claims covered by CPR Part 57, for example, probate claims (claims concerning the validity of a Will), claims for the rectification of a Will and claims for the substitution or removal of a personal representative.[37]

As a general point it is worth considering that once proceedings are within the ambit of Part 7 the costs may go higher.

What is the Legal Procedure?

Following service of the claim form via Part 8[38], the defendants have 14 days to acknowledge service stating whether they intend to contest the claim and whether they seek a separate remedy. At the same time, they are expected to file their written evidence.

An extension of time can be agreed for serving and filing written evidence provided it is not more than 14 days after the acknowledgement of service. Such agreement must be filed with the court with the acknowledgment of service.

37 CPR 57.1

38 N208

A claimant has an additional 14 days to file written evidence in reply to that filed by the defendant. This time can be extended by agreement to up to 28 days from service of the defendant's evidence.[39]

Trusts

One of the potential fraud issues relate to trust which we cover now.

It is worth looking at the obligation of trustees.

What Are the legal obligations of trustees?

1. To exercise reasonable care and skill

Section 1 of the Trustee Act 2000 provides a general duty of care that is applicable to both trustees and PRs. The duty applies to specific situations defined in the Act, such as investing trust funds or acquiring land. Where the duty applies, a trustee must use such care and skill as is reasonable in the circumstances.

For trustees with professional knowledge or trustees acting in the course of business, i.e. professional trustees, a higher standard of care will be expected, in line with their additional knowledge.

In addition, there is a common law duty of care to act in the best interests of the beneficiaries even if this conflicts with the trustee's personal beliefs.

The standard of care applicable is that expected of a prudent businessman managing affairs for someone he felt morally bound to provide for and depends on the individual's skills and expertise.

---

39 CPR 8.5

The Will or trust instrument may exclude the duty of care and may exclude trustees' liability for breach of duty.

2. To act in the best interests of the beneficiaries as a whole

- Trustees should not favour one beneficiary over the others. This means that they should maintain a balance between the beneficiaries. For example, trustees of a life interest trust should not prefer the interests of the remainderman over those of the life tenant or vice versa.[40]

- Where the testator or settlor had a personal connection to the life tenant but not to the remainderman, the PRs or trustees can prefer the interests of the beneficiary known to the testator of settler to a certain extent. This does not, however, allow them to exclude the interests of the remainderman entirely (Nestlé v. National Westminster Bank plc [1993] 1 WLR 1260). Duties and Responsibilities of Trustees and Personal Representatives.

- Not to be remunerated for services provided unless authorised.

- It is common now for a Will or trust instrument to provide for PRs and trustees, particularly professionals, to be paid.

- A professional PR or trustee can be paid if all his fellow PRs or trustees agree in writing, even if the Will or trust instrument does not specify this (s.29(2) Trustee Act 2000). This provision does not apply to sole PRs or trustees or to charity trustees. A sole PR or trustee of a non-charitable trust will therefore need to appoint

---

40 Lloyds Bank plc v Duker [1987] 1 WLR 1324 where it was held that shares in a private company should not be divided between the beneficiaries as this would give one beneficiary control of the company and therefore favour him beyond what the testator had intended.

a co-trustee to receive remuneration if this is not expressly authorised by the Will or Trust Instrument.

- Not to use trust property for private advantage. A trustee may not sell trust property to himself nor make a secret profit from the trust as there is a conflict between the trustee's fiduciary duty and his personal interest.[41]

3. To obey the terms of the trust

In the case of a Will trust, the terms will normally be found in the Will.

If trustees act outside the terms they will be in breach of trust.[42]

4. To invest trust funds properly

Trustees have a duty to preserve the trust fund which implies a duty to invest any money not required for current use. This includes a duty to convert any improper funds into sensible assets, e.g. to convert investments in a life interest trust which only produce capital to income producing investments.

Trustees should obtain the best rate of return available.

The Trustee Act 2000 provides trustees with a general power of investment to invest as if they were absolutely entitled to the assets of the trust.

---

41 Re Thompson's Settlement [1986] Ch 99 where it was held that a transaction involving two trustees could not stand once it had been called into question by a beneficiary.

42 Target Holdings Ltd v Redferns [1996] AC 421 at 434 where it was held that a solicitor who was holding a lender's money on trust for completion of a purchase but paid the money out 10 days beforehand was in breach of trust.

Before exercising their powers of investment, trustees must obtain and consider proper advice on the suitability of the proposed investment unless they reasonably conclude that in all the circumstances it is unnecessary or inappropriate to do so.

Trustees must also review their investments from time to time to consider whether they should be varied considering the standard investment criteria.

What are key problem areas?

Accounts?

Executors (who are not necessarily trustees) do not have a duty to inform beneficiaries of their interests, the distinction being that a Will is a public document. However, in the case of a Will establishing a trust, assuming the executors and trustees are the same people, once the administration of the estate is complete the executors will become trustees and will then have a duty to inform beneficiaries of their interests.

A trustee must keep clear and accurate accounts (Springett v Dashwood (1860) 2 Giff 521).

A beneficiary theoretically has the right to see the accounts (Armitage v Nurse [1998] Ch 241).

A beneficiary does not have the right to be given other information about the trust but may apply to the Court for an Order requiring the trustees to produce this information. He or she is likely to be granted access to the information if his or her request is reasonable, as in Schmidt v. Rosewood Trust [2003] UKPC 26).

Trust accounts

If you are dealing with a fraud situation it is highly likely that you will focus on accounts.

Trustees have a duty to keep clear trust accounts and to be constantly ready with those accounts. "Being ready" with the accounts is important and trustees who are slow in producing accounts are likely to be penalised in costs (West v Lazard Brothers [No 1] [1987-88] JLR 414). Therefore, if a beneficiary requests a copy of the trust accounts, the trustees should provide a copy. If they do not, the beneficiary can seek the accounts via the court, and the court usually orders the trustees to pay personally (not from the trust fund) the costs of obtaining the order.

If a beneficiary seeks disclosure of trust accounts apparently in order to attack the trust or trust property (such as a challenge to the validity of the trust which would be against the interests of the beneficiaries as a whole) the trustees ought to be cautious. If the trustees are unsure of the reason for the request, they should clarify that with the beneficiary before making a decision. However, there is a strong presumption in favour of disclosure. The trustees' concerns can usually be relieved by obtaining a confidentiality undertaking from the beneficiary that restricts the use of the accounts in other proceedings.

Henchley v Thompson [2017] EWHC 225 (Ch), where the court ordered the defendant to provide an account to the beneficiaries of his dealings with a trust of which he had been a trustee (or de facto trustee) up to the early 1990s, is reminder that the duty to account to beneficiaries is a core duty and can still be relevant after many years.

In the case of Lewis v Tamplin ([2018] EWHC 777 Ch) the London High Court was asked to exercise its jurisdiction to supervise trustees in the performance of their obligations by requiring trustees to give disclosure of documents requested by certain beneficiaries. The case also serves as a reminder of the rules regarding privilege between trustees and beneficiaries. We consider this case further below.

In some circumstances, it may be appropriate for trustees to limit the information provided to a beneficiary. For example, where there are sub-funds, it may be appropriate to ensure that the beneficiary sees only the information relating to the sub-fund in which he has an interest.

The Judge emphasised that beneficiaries have a right to hold trustees to account and to ask them for information regarding the performance of their obligations under the trust. If the trustees refuse to divulge such information then the beneficiaries can ask the Court to order the disclosure of documents containing the information, using the Court's inherent jurisdiction to supervise trustees in performance of their obligations. However, if a request is made for information which is not in documentary form then it is not certain that an order for disclosure will be made. First, the beneficiaries would have to meet the cost of turning the information into a documentary form. Secondly, beneficiaries are not entitled to receive information regarding "why" a trustee made certain decisions.

Trustees need to carefully consider whether to disclose information, and remember that the Court can order the disclosure of information using its inherent jurisdiction.

Trustees should also note that beneficiaries do not have to prove that there is a "real suspicion", but rather the Court will decide whether it is proper for them to interfere.

Additionally trustees are reminded that the Court may not view it positively if disclosures are only made begrudgingly and upon the imminent threat of legal action.

From the perspective of beneficiaries, they must ensure that document requests are framed properly and not overly wide or seeking information (as opposed to documents).

Appropriate delegation?

The Trustee Act 2000 (s.11) allows trustees to appoint agents to exercise any of their delegable functions. The functions that trustees are not allowed to delegate include: any function relating to whether or in what way any assets of the trust should be distributed.

For both estate and trust administration, there exists a clear duty to ascertain the assets and liabilities, and to administer these according to the terms of the will or trust deed, and the law. Appropriate records should therefore be maintained which will enable them to successfully do so.

What documents should be retained?

For an estate administration, the main documents to retain must include the Will and Codicils (where applicable); the original sealed Grant of Representation (plus copies); any Instruments of Variation; original death certificates; and copy birth or marriage certificates for beneficiaries whose entitlements are determined by age, or those who have married since execution of the Will.

The same approach to record-keeping applies to the administration of trusts. A trust may arise out of an estate administration, and therefore the retention of the above documents will also be essential in ensuring that an ongoing trust is administered appropriately from the outset.

Trustees must be familiar with the terms of the trust (Hallows v Lloyd (1888)), and must be prepared to produce on request any documents or information about the trust, including the trust deed as in Manning v Commissioner of Taxation (1928).

How Do You Go About Attacking the Conduct of an Errant Trustee?

The Trust instrument

First focus on the trust instrument. This is a key document, which trustees should disclose to beneficiaries if requested. The same applies to supplemental documents such as:

- Deeds of appointment and retirement of trustees.
- Instruments adding assets to the trust.
- Instruments varying the trust.

Focus on the legislation

Trustees can also be removed without the court's intervention by fellow trustees if one or more of many conditions is met. These conditions are set out in s.36 Trustee Act 1925 which provides:

> "*(1) Where a trustee, either original or substituted, and whether appointed by a court or otherwise, is dead or remains out of the United Kingdom for more than twelve months, or desires to be discharged from all or any of the trusts or powers reposed in or conferred on him, or refuses or is unfit to act therein, or is incapable of acting therein, or is an infant, then, subject to the restrictions imposed by this Act on the number of trustees, —*
>
> *(a) the person or persons nominated for the purpose of appointing new trustees by the instrument, if any, creating the trust; or*
>
> *(b) if there is no such persons, or no such person able and willing to act, then the surviving or continuing trustees or trustee for the time being, or the personal representatives of the last surviving or continuing trustee; may, by writing, appoint one or more other persons (whether or not being the persons exercising the power) to be a trustee or trustees*

> *in the place of the trustee so deceased, remaining out of the United Kingdom, desiring to be discharged, refusing, or being unfit or being incapable, or being an infant, as aforesaid.*"

Also consider s.36 (9) Trustee Act 1925 which lays down that where a trustee who lacks capacity is also a beneficiary of the trust then it is necessary to make an application for that person's removal to the Court of Protection; the court which deals with matters of physical and mental welfare.

How to Prove That the Trustee Is Unfit?

This can be very subjective and will be disputed. Being 'unfit' depends on the circumstances of the case.

Generally, a person who has been made bankrupt or convicted of a fraudulent offence will most likely be deemed to be unfit to act as will a trustee guilty of a significant breach of trust or of acting in a way which causes a conflict as between their personal position and their duty to the beneficiaries, known as their 'fiduciary duty'.

Even if a trustee is removed under s.36 Trustee Act 1925, it is entirely possible that they could challenge such a decision by way of court action.

Further, as is clear from s.36 Trustee Act 1925, this remedy is not automatically available to beneficiaries unless they are also trustees or they have power to remove trustees under the trust instrument.

What are the legal ways to remove a trustee?

The court can remove a trustee either by statutory power (under s.41 Trustee Act 1925) or under its inherent authority.

s.41(1) Trustee Act 1925 provides:

> "*The court may, whenever it is expedient to appoint a new trustee or new trustees, and it is found inexpedient difficult or impracticable so to do without the assistance of the court, make an order appointing a new trustee or new trustees either in substitution for or in addition to any existing trustee or trustees, or although there is no existing trustee.*
>
> *In particular and without prejudice to the generality of the foregoing provision, the court may make an order appointing a new trustee in substitution for a trustee who lacks capacity to exercise his functions as trustee, or is a bankrupt, or is a corporation which is in liquidation or has been dissolved.*"

As such, and assuming there is no other method open to a party to remove a trustee, the court may do so under s.41 Trustee Act 1925 where a trustee lacks capacity, is bankrupt or, if a corporation, in liquidation or has been dissolved.

If seeking to remove a trustee under s.41 Trustee Act 1925, you should ensure you have a replacement or substitute trustee available and that trustee should file at court what is known as a 'consent to act'; a witness statement confirming the proposed replacement trustee's agreement to act as a trustee.

This should be filed along with a 'fitness to act'; a statement by somebody who knows the trustee and can vouch for their standing and suitability to act as a trustee.[43]

One way to remove a trustee is to rely on an express provision in the trust instrument. This provision may either be a power of removal, or a provision for the automatic removal of a trustee.

The court has an inherent jurisdiction to replace or remove a trustee (although it will not remove a trustee without a replacement if there is

---

[43] cf Letterstedt v Broers (1884) 9 App Cas 371

not a sufficient number of trustees remaining, should the removal in question take place). Ordinarily, there should be at least two trustees of a trust, but the trust instrument may set out a minimum or maximum number of trustees.

Each case will be considered on its own facts.

A key case is Letterstedt v Broers (1884) 9 App Cas 371 in which Lord Blackburn, sitting in the South African court, said

> "*the acts or omissions must be such as to endanger the trust property or to shew a want of honesty, or a want of proper capacity to execute the duties, or a want of reasonable fidelity*";
>
> "*It must always be borne in mind that trustees exist for the benefit of those to whom the creator of the trust estate has given the trust estate*"; and
>
> "*friction or hostility between trustees and the immediate possessor of the trust estate is not of itself a reason for the removal of the trustees. But where the hostility is grounded on the mode in which the trust has been administered.,. It is certainly not to be disregarded.*"

Breaking the trust

Another method which can achieve the same aims is to break the trust.

The principle is laid down in the case of Saunders v Vaultier (1841) Cr & Ph 240, which should be familiar to most trust and estate lawyers, and confirms that beneficiaries who are over 18, have capacity and, together, are absolutely entitled to the trust property i.e. unanimous, can 'break the trust'.

This mirrors the language of s.19 Trusts of Land and Appointment of Trustees Act 1996.

In short, this means that the beneficiaries can bring the trust to an end and take their respective shares or, in the case of a life interest or discretionary trust, agree amongst themselves how much each should receive.

How should trustees deal with requests for information by beneficiaries?

If a beneficiary requests information about the trust, the trustees should bear in mind that the beneficiary has no entitlement as of right. The trustees have discretion and should conduct a balancing exercise, considering all the relevant circumstances at the time. They should consider what is in the best interests of the beneficiaries as a whole. They should also consider what the purpose of the request is. Whether or not they decide to exercise their discretion to disclose may depend on the type of document requested.

Legal Proceedings

Proceedings under s. 41 of the Trustee Act 1925 should normally be commenced by a Part 8 claim form [44] (on the basis that there is no substantial dispute of fact).

All the trustees should be parties. The beneficiaries should also be joined, unless perhaps they have consented to the application. The settlor (if alive) and any person nominated to appoint new trustees should also be joined.

If there is a substantial dispute of fact, the proceedings should be brought pursuant to the inherent jurisdiction of the court by way of a Part 7 claim form. However, those proceedings may include a claim for the

---

44 https://www.justice.gov.uk/courts/procedure-rules/civil/rules/part64

appointment of new trustees pursuant to s. 41 of the Trustee Act 1925. The proceedings should be brought in the Chancery Division of the High Court (unless the value of the trust fund does not exceed £100,000, in which case it can be brought in the County Court).

When considering an application under section 41 of the Trustee Act 1925 the court used to object to the appointment of a beneficiary unless this could not be avoided (Re Harrop's Trust (1882) 24 Ch.D. 717 and Re Paines Trusts (1885) 33 WR 564) but, these days, if no independent trustee is available the court often appoints beneficiaries. However, the court is unlikely to appoint beneficiaries that are unwilling to act or where it is going to be difficult for a particular beneficiary to manage inherent conflicts of interest.

The application may be made by a beneficiary or a trustee (s. 58 of the Trustee Act 1925). The jurisdiction does not apply to personal representatives (s. 41(4)). However, there is a separate jurisdiction relating to the appointment and removal of personal representatives under section 50 of the Administration of Justice Act 1985 which we cover in a separate chapter.

The court has power to appoint a new trustee or trustees in substitution for any existing trustee or trustees provided that (a) it is expedient to make the appointment and (b) it is inexpedient, difficult or impracticable to do so without the assistance of the court. The court, therefore, has a statutory power to remove a trustee, but only in conjunction with the appointment of a new trustee or trustees.

Some Useful Case law for Combatting Trustees

Trustees should firstly consider whether the person requesting information is entitled to the information or documentation. It is long established that trustees should inform adult beneficiaries who have an interest in possession, that is, the right to income from the trust assets or a right to use trust assets about the existence of the trust and the nature of their interest in the trust (Brittlebank v Goodwin [1868]).[45]

Even where a beneficiary only has a potential future interest under the trust, trustees should consider notifying beneficiaries of the existence of the trust and their prospective interest. This includes beneficiaries who are likely to benefit under a discretionary trust (per Chaine-Nickson v Bank of Ireland [1976]).[46]

In Re Londonderry's Settlement [1964] a case regarding a discretionary trust and the right to disclosure of trust documents the court considered what were and were not trust documents and identified documents that a beneficiary was or was not entitled to disclosure of. It was held that the right to disclosure covered only documents relating to the ownership, management or administration of any property vested in the trustees.

In Long v Rodman, Chief Master Marsh emphasised that the court's discretion to remove a trustee (or as was the case, an executor) is to be exercised in a pragmatic way.

In Schmidt v Rosewood Trust Limited [2003] a case regarding an Isle of Man discretionary trust, the son of the settlor requested disclosure of trust documents by virtue of his discretionary interest and his expectation of benefitting under the discretionary trust settlements and because he was administrator of the settlor's estate.

The Privy Council held that no beneficiary is entitled or has a right to disclosure of trust documents and that disclosure to a beneficiary is not dependent on the beneficiary having a proprietary interesting the trust assets. The court went on to say that beneficiaries could seek disclosure

45 LR 5 Eq 545]

46 IR 393)

of trust documents using the court's inherent jurisdiction to supervise and if necessary to intervene in the administration of trusts.

However, the court also held that "... no beneficiary (and least of all a discretionary object) has any entitlement as of right to disclosure of anything which can plausibly be described as a trust document. ... when there are issues as to personal or commercial confidentiality, the court may have to balance the competing interests of different beneficiaries, the trustees themselves, and third parties. Disclosure may have to be limited and safeguards may have to be put in place. Evaluation of the claims of a beneficiary (and especially of a discretionary object) may be an important part of the balancing exercise which the court has to perform on the materials placed before it. In many cases the court may have no difficulty in concluding that an applicant with no more than a theoretical possibility of benefit ought not to be granted any relief."

Bank Statements

A key area for participants is the obtaining of bank statements.

This can involve ultimately complaining to financial institutions.

Businesses regulated by the Financial Conduct Authority "must treat their customers fairly."

If you think you've been treated unfairly you can complain, first to the company, then – if you're not satisfied – you can escalate it to the Financial Ombudsman Service.

It is worth noting that:

- The Financial Ombudsman Service's range is huge – covering areas most of us deal with in our daily lives. Its remit includes bank accounts, credit cards, debt collection, irresponsible lending, car finance, PPI, investments, mortgages and loans, pensions and savings. See more below on how the ombudsman can help you.

- You must complain directly to the company before you complain to the ombudsman. A business has eight weeks to consider your complaint and give you a "final response".

- The best way to complain to the ombudsman is via its online form. The ombudsman has a "complaint checker" where you answer some initial questions about your complaint. Once you've done this, it'll take you to the relevant form.

Self dealing rule

Another potential area of Elderly fraud is on executors and trustees self dealing.

It can be quite common for a lay Executor to wish to purchase property from an Estate particularly where that Executor is also a beneficiary.

An Executor owes a fiduciary duty to the beneficiaries of an estate. This means that they must act solely in the best interests of the beneficiaries. An Executor is, therefore, prohibited from making a profit from the estate and putting themselves in a position where their interests conflict with their duties as an Executor.

The self-dealing rule applies where an Executor or Trustee wishes to either buy an estate or trust asset or where a Trustee sells their own property to the trust. Transactions of this type are contrary to the duty to avoid conflict of interests and duty not to exploit a fiduciary position for profit.

A beneficiary can set the transaction aside unless the Executor, according to the case of Tito v Waddel, No.2) [1977] can show they have not taken advantage of their position, they have made a full disclosure to the beneficiaries and the transaction is fair and honest.

The self-dealing rule operates strictly and as noted in Tito v Waddell (the rule is 'a severe one which will apply however honest the circumstances and fair the price'.

Executors should also take care when selling an asset to a buyer who is related to them in some way.

In Tito v. Waddell (No 2), Sir Robert Megarry V-C distinguished between two rules applicable to trustees. The first, which he called the 'self dealing rule', is that 'if a trustee purchases trust property from himself, any beneficiary may have the sale set aside ex debito justitiae, however fair the transaction.'

The second, labelled the 'fair-dealing rule', is that 'if a trustee purchases his beneficiary's beneficial interest, the beneficiary may have the sale set aside unless the trustee can establish the propriety of the transaction, showing that he had taken no advantage of his position and that the beneficiary was fully informed and received full value.'

The traditional approach of the court is that a trustee is not entitled to acquire trust property, if even a single beneficiary objects, notwithstanding that the trustee did not, in fact, take advantage of his office and the price is a fair one (Re Thompson's Settlement [1986] Ch 99).

Court Authorisation In more modern times it has, however, been accepted that the self-dealing rule is not absolute, and that the court has a discretion to authorise a self-dealing transaction either prospectively or retrospectively (Mills v Mills [2015] EWHC 1522 (Ch).

An application for court authorisation may be particularly appropriate where there are unborn, minor or untraceable beneficiaries who cannot give their consent.

However, the court also has a discretion to permit a self-dealing in the face of objections from a beneficiary (Holder v Holder [1968] Ch 353, at 398 and 402). The self-dealing transaction will only be authorised or allowed to stand in exceptional circumstances.

In Holder v Holder an executor had sold estate land to himself. The sale was not set aside, but only because the executor had only carried out minor acts of administration before attempting to renounce.

In Hall v Peck [2011] WTLR 605 the self-dealing rule was applied with full force at the instance of an objecting beneficiary. The rule applied unless it could be shown that any detriment to the estate was either non-existent or de minimis, and such as to be outweighed by, or otherwise not to justify, the consequences of setting aside the transaction.

CHAPTER NINE

LASTING POWERS OF ATTORNEY, COURT OF PROTECTION AND DEPUTYSHIP FRAUD

Introduction

For information about Lasting Power of Attorneys please consider the relevant of my previous book[47] or go online to the government website.[48]

In addition, there is information on Enduring Power of Attorney.[49] There is also useful background online about the Court of Protection[50] and the Office of Public Guardian[51] and Deputies.[52]

By reading this largely succinct information you have an understanding of the principle at play.

---

47 https://www.lawbriefpublishing.com/elderlylaw

48 https://www.gov.uk/power-of-attorney

49 https://www.gov.uk/enduring-power-attorney-duties

50 https://www.gov.uk/courts-tribunals/court-of-protection

51 https://www.gov.uk/government/organisations/office-of-the-public-guardian

52 https://www.gov.uk/become-deputy

The Office of the Public Guardian

The Public Guardian is responsible under the Mental Capacity Act for:

- supervising deputies appointed by the Court of Protection.

- keeping registers of deputies, Lasting Powers of Attorney, and Enduring Powers of Attorney; and

- investigating any complaints about attorneys or deputies.

Who can make applications to the Court?

Anyone can make an application if they feel they have just cause. Usually people making applications will be:

- vulnerable adults who feel they have been unfairly determined as lacking capacity to decide

- family members who disagree amongst themselves or with an agency about what's in the best interests of the person lacking capacity

- family or friends who wish to seek authority to manage the affairs of a person who is lacking capacity to make decisions about their own affairs

- NHS Trusts which need to make a major decision about serious medical treatment for a person who lacks capacity

- local authorities which have concerns about major decisions affecting the person's welfare

Some Quick Options to Resolve Problems With Attorneys[53]

- Inform the relevant local authority as its social services department can investigate whether an attorney is an appropriate person to have access to a vulnerable person.
- Tell the police if intentional abuse is suspected, as this falls under fraud and theft. They can investigate and refer the matter to the Crown Prosecution Service.
- Contact the Office of the Public Guardian, which regulates and oversees all attorneys.

How do you apply to the Court of Protection?

When considering welfare decisions, attorneys and/or deputies, and anyone else involved in P's care, should try and resolve welfare issues involving P at a 'best interests meeting'. Applying to the Court of Protection should be a last resort.

Applications are also made to the Court of Protection for the court to appoint a 'deputy' (if P has not already appointed an attorney), as well as for applications regarding P's finances, such as the approval to make gifts or to approve an investment.

How long do applications to the Court of Protection take?

The Court of Protection deals with both contested and non-contested applications and the time it will take to resolve an application with vary

[53] You and your clients should be careful before jumping in and approaching relevant bodies as if this goes to Court can be deemed over-aggressive. The least expensive way to resolve a case is for a third party to do the work for you and your client but be careful as to what that can achieve.

depending on which one is made. Most non-contested and straightforward applications, such as deputyship applications, are dealt with on paper without the need for the applicant to attend a hearing. A final order is usually made within four to six months.

Contested applications (which is what you are looking at in a fraud situation), which arise when someone objects to an application, will almost always be the subject of a hearing. Such applications often concern the validity of a lasting power of attorney, the removal of an attorney or deputy as a result of their misconduct, or disputed terms in a proposed statutory will.

Early Stage Objections[54]

There are two different types of LPA; Property and Financial Affairs, and Health and Welfare.[55]

A Property and Financial Affairs LPA gives an attorney the power to make decisions in regards to money and property.

A Health and Welfare LPA gives an attorney the power to make decisions in regards to a range of things such as medical care, moving into a care home and life sustaining treatment. A Health and Welfare can only be used if the donor has been deemed to have lost mental capacity by a professional.

Relatives will not automatically be notified when somebody is appointed as an individual's attorney. It is the donor's decision as to whether they wish to notify anybody and these people will be named in the LPA as a

---

54 https://www.gov.uk/object-registration-power-attorney

55 An online tool to apply for Lasting Power of Attorney (LPA) is still not available despite being announced in 2023. This means the paper form remains the only way to apply for this crucial protection.

person to be notified. The person to be notified will receive a letter advising them that the donor is making a particular type of LPA and who they are appointing as their attorneys. If the donor does not include anybody to be notified, then the only people who will be automatically aware of the LPA are the people named in the LPA, as they will need to sign the document.

Who can object to an appointment?

If someone has been listed as a person to be notified they will receive a document from the Office of the Public Guardian informing them that the donor is planning to register the LPA and who the nominated attorneys will be. The person who has been notified then has the opportunity to object to the LPA. Their objection can be based on either 'factual objection' or 'objection on prescribed grounds'.

Someone can object based on factual objection if they have been listed as a person to be notified and:

- The donor or an attorney has died
- The donor and the attorney were married or were in a civil partnership and have now divorced
- An attorney who has been chosen does not have mental capacity
- An attorney has chosen to stop acting as attorney
- The donor or an attorney has become bankrupt.

In order to object based on factual objection, the person to be notified must object within three weeks of receiving the notification of registration.

Someone can object based on prescribed grounds if the LPA has already been made and they believe:

- The LPA isn't legally correct
- They don't believe the donor had the mental capacity to make an LPA
- The donor cancelled their LPA when they regained capacity
- There was fraud, e.g., someone forged the donor's signature
- The donor was pressured into making the LPA
- An attorney is acting against the donor's best interests.
- In order to object based on prescribed grounds, the person notified must be able to provide evidence to support their objection.

Another final way to object to the LPA is if the donor believes that the attorney is unsuitable. In this situation the donor can complete a form to send to the Office of Public Guardian.

Latter Stages Objections

Grounds for the revocation of an LPA with supporting evidence

Another way to contest a Power of Attorney is providing supporting evidence on prescribed grounds where:

- The LPA isn't legally correct
- The donor did not have the mental capacity to make an LPA
- The donor revoked their LPA when they regained capacity
- There was fraud
- The donor was pressured or coerced into making the LPA

- An attorney is acting against the donor's best interests.

Examples of supportive evidence include medical records, capacity assessments or the recollections of the donor's family or caregivers from when the LPA was executed.

Process for handling power of attorney challenges

The relevant forms for objections can be found on the gov.uk website.[56] Once submitted, the objector will be contacted by the OPG or Court of Protection to advise if they have enough information to proceed or if a hearing is needed.

If there are concerns about the LPA after it has been registered, the first step would be to set out your concerns to the OPG. They will then see if they have the legal authority to investigate. If the donor is alive, then generally, they will they will investigate matters but be wary of the time frames that they take to deal with matters.

Enduring Power of Attorney

The Court of Protection can only remove an attorney under a registered enduring power of attorney (EPA) on the following grounds ((paragraph 16(4) of schedule 4 to the Mental Capacity Act 2005 (MCA 2005)):

- Fraud or undue pressure was put on the donor to create the EPA
- Having regard to all the circumstances, and in particular the attorney's relationship to or connection with the donor, the attorney is unsuitable to be the donor's attorney

56 https://www.gov.uk/object-registration-power-attorney

General provisions

The statutory jurisdiction for the removal of an attorney appointed by LPA is found in section 22 of the MCA. The Court of Protection may direct that an instrument purporting to be an LPA is not to be registered or that it is to revoked (if P lacks capacity to do so), where the execution or creation of the LPA has been procured by fraud or undue pressure (s23(4)(a)) or where the donee has behaved or is proposing to behave in a way that would contravene his authority or is not, or would not be, in P's best interests (s23(4)(b)).

The jurisdiction in relation to the appointment, removal or supervision of deputies is derived from section 16 of the MCA.

Grounds for revoking an LPA

Under section 22(3) of the Mental Capacity Act 2005, the Court of Protection may revoke a LPA if it is satisfied that:

- fraud or undue pressure was used to induce the Donor to create the LPA; or
- the attorney of the LPA:
    - has behaved, or is behaving, in a way that contravenes his authority or is not in the Donor's best interests; or
    - proposes to behave in a way that would contravene his authority or would not be in the Donor's best interests.

Revoking an LPA is a serious step and the Court of Protection will look at all the circumstances, including the gravity of the offending or prospective behaviours. The Court will also consider whether it is necessary and proportionate to revoke an LPA and ultimately, whether the revocation would be in the Donor's best interests.

The following cases show the approach taken by the Court of Protection in deciding on revocation.

The Public Guardian v CS & PL [2015] EWCOP30

The Donor, EL, was diagnosed with vascular dementia in 2009 and appointed her two children, CS, and PL, as her attorneys with the power to act jointly in relation to the sale of her house and jointly and severally for all other decisions. The LPA was registered on 12 July 2010.

The attorneys' relationship broke down due to differing views on who should control EL's finances. They each made complaints to the Office of the Public Guardian and accused each other of misconduct. This led to PL making an application to the Court of Protection in December 2012 to revoke the LPA and for PL to be appointed as sole deputy for EL's finances. By that time, it was apparent that EL had lost the capacity to revoke her LPA.0000.

It became clear to Senior Judge Lush that the LPA was not functioning properly due to the animosity between the attorneys and the refusal to respect the Schedule of Agreed Responsibilities. They had also delegated their responsibilities to their father.

In addition, the Judge was of the view that the attorneys made gifts to themselves from EL's funds which were far more than what they could do under section 12 of the Mental Capacity Act 2005. As a result, the Judge was satisfied that both attorneys behaved in a way that contravened their authority and was not in EL's best interests. The Judge ordered the revocation of the LPA and invited a panel deputy to apply to be appointed as EL's deputy for property and affairs.

A subsequent case regarding the revocation of LPAs followed only a month later and was heard by the same Judge.

Re GM [2013][57]

Senior Judge Lush set out the parameters of "reasonable" gifting by Deputies. This case clarifies that the authority of deputies and attorneys to make gifts is limited without the court's consent. Re GM is a clear example of financial abuse by joint deputies that did not go unnoticed by the Office of the Public Guardian (OPG). One of the main jobs of the OPG is to supervise deputies appointed by the Court of Protection and it is reassuring to know that the OPG will notice such cases of excessive expenditure and refer the matter to the Court of Protection.

In Re GM, the judge found that the deputies were personally liable to G's estate and were ordered to repay £205,000. The joint deputyship appointments were revoked. The judge ordered that somebody 'with experience of unjust enrichment and restitution' be appointed in their place. In other words, a professional deputy should be appointed who could take the necessary legal action against the former deputies to enforce the court's order for repayment.

Legal Options

The key objective for Court of Protection lawyers and their clients will be in to stop the abuse and then give consideration to whether or not any remedies need to be sought to rectify the consequences of the abuse.

For probate practitioners, the main issue will be whether or not any proceedings should be brought to recover the proceeds of financial abuse

57 Re GM: MJ v JM The Public Guardian [2013] EWCOP 2966.

in the interests of maximising the deceased person's estate or enabling a beneficiary to make a claim.

Challenging a LPA

The Court of Protection has power to consider "any questions relating to whether the power has been revoked or has otherwise end" (MCA 2005, s 22 (2) (b).

The Public Guardian may apply to the Court of Protection in serious cases (MCA Code of Practice 7.72) where the donor may have been subject to abuse or where there is a report that the donor may have been subject to undue influence or fraud in the creation of the power of the LPA.

Where it is satisfied that an attorney proposes to behave, has behaved, in a way that contravenes the donor's authority or is not in the donor's best interests, the court has discretion if another attorney is authorised to act jointly and severally can continue to act or the terms of the power allow for the appointment of a replacement attorney, to partially revoke the power as far as it relates the appointment of that attorney (MCA 2005 s 22 (5)).

The court can only exercise its power to revoke, or partially revoke, the power if the donor lacks capacity to revoke for him/herself. (MCA ss 22 (4) (b).

Can you Remove the Attorney?

For the grounds for removing an attorney under a registered LPA the Court of Protection can make an order for revocation of an LPA in relation to one or all attorneys, on the following grounds please consider the MCA 2005 s 22(4)(b).[58]

These are in addition to the right of the Court to declare that the LPA was invalidly created or has been revoked and should thus be removed from the register.

When considering whether to remove an attorney, the Court takes the fact that the donor appointed that person to be their attorney as an important written expression of the donor's wishes and feelings regarding who should manage their funds (Re RG [2015] EWCOP 2).

Further, where the Court has concerns about an attorney, but is of the view that those concerns can be mitigated by closer supervision, it can

---

[58] 22 Powers of court in relation to validity of lasting powers of attorney

(2) The court may determine any question relating to—

(a) whether one or more of the requirements for the creation of a lasting power of attorney have been met;

(b) whether the power has been revoked or has otherwise come to an end.

(3) Subsection (4) applies if the court is satisfied—

(a) that fraud or undue pressure was used to induce P—

(i) to execute an instrument for the purpose of creating a lasting power of attorney, or

(ii) to create a lasting power of attorney, or

(b) that the donee (or, if more than one, any of them) of a lasting power of attorney—

(i) has behaved, or is behaving, in a way that contravenes his authority or is not in P's best interests, or

(ii) proposes to behave in a way that would contravene his authority or would not be in P's best interests revoke the LPA and appoint the attorney as a deputy (Re AMH [2015] EWCOP 70).

When considering whether an attorney has behaved in a way that is contrary to the best interests of P, the court can consider the attorney's behaviour in the wider world, not just in their role as attorney (Re J (unreported), 6 December 2010, CoP).

Similarly to attorneys acting under an EPA, where attorneys are unable to work together to the extent that they are unable to operate the LPA for the purpose that it was intended, they may not be acting in the donor's best interests, which is a ground for the court to revoke the LPA (Re EL (revoking a lasting power of attorney) [2015] EWCOP 30).

The Court can also make a proactive removal of an attorney when they are proposing to act in a way that contravenes their authority or is inconsistent with the donor's best interests (Re KC [2020] EWCOP 62).[59]

Deputyship

The CoP has authority to remove a deputy under section 16(8) of the MCA 2005, and the wording and grounds mirror that of removal under an LPA. In addition, a deputy can be removed if they act inconsistently with the wording of the Order. Therefore, careful attention must be given to the wording and also the reporting requirements of a deputy.

---

59 Applying to the Court of Protection: an application to remove an attorney must be made to the Court of Protection. The application should include a COP1 form (an application form) and a COP3 form (an assessment of capacity). It should outline the reasons for the application and demonstrate that the individual concerned lacks the capacity to make the decision to remove the attorney themselves.

Whilst each case is different, the approach the Court takes is likely to have the following starting point (Re B (unreported, 15 August 2011):

- An application for the removal of a deputy may be made by any interested person, including P;
- The burden of proof is on the person seeking a change in the status quo, on the usual civil standard;
- A reason for the change of status quo must usually be given;
- If there is no assertion that the existing deputy is unsuitable, or the applicant fails to prove that the existing deputy is unsuitable, strong evidence is needed that it is in P's best interests to discharge the existing deputy and appoint a new one, in accordance with s.4 MCA 2005.

In the case of Kambli v The Public Guardian [2021] EWCOP 53 (27 August 2021), the Court confirmed:

> "*When a deputyship encounters difficulties, the response of the Court should not be to change the appointment as default response. Changing deputy inevitably incurs costs which could otherwise be avoided and risks being perceived as 'rewarding' negative behaviour, which in turn undermines the prospects of future stability. Rather the Court should probe the actual circumstances, with a view to salvaging working relationships if possible.*"

As with attorneyship, P's wishes and feelings will be a key consideration (Essex CC v CVF [2020] EWCOP 65).

EPA

The statutory jurisdiction for the removal of an attorney appointed by EPA is found in paragraph 16 of Schedule 4 MCA 2005. The "misconduct" ground for revocation is in paragraph 16(4)(g). The Court must direct the Public Guardian to cancel the registration of an EPA "on being satisfied that, having regard to all the circumstances, and in particular the attorney's relationship to or connection with the donor, the attorney is unsuitable to be the donor's attorney".

The role of the local authority

Local authorities have statutory safeguarding duties in relation to adults in their area at risk of abuse, including financial abuse.

The statutory framework, and the precise criteria for investigation, differs depending upon whether the adult is in England (where the framework is the Care Act 2014) or Wales (where it is the Social Services and Well-being (Wales) Act 2014). However, in both cases, the local authority must either itself or through others make such enquiries as are necessary to decide whether action should be taken, and, if so, by whom.

Each local authority has adult safeguarding officers who may also be known as (vulnerable) adult protection officers, with responsibility to involve multi-agency teams and manage cases referred to them.

The precise scope of the enquiry, who leads it and its nature, and how long it takes, will depend on the particular circumstances. The local authority is then under a duty to decide what – if any – further action is to be taken.

There is detailed statutory guidance applying to local authorities in the discharge of their safeguarding duties for England and Wales. There will be statutory guidance under the Domestic Abuse Act 2021, which sets out local authorities responsibilities for safeguarding and supporting victims of domestic abuse.

Abuse and neglect by legal professionals

If you suspect abuse or neglect by another legal professional, you should contact the SRA professional ethics helpline for guidance.

Criminal offences

If you suspect a criminal offence may be taking place, contact your local authority adult safeguarding team or the police, phoning the number 101.

However, the police may ask that no action be taken while they investigate and gather evidence against the perpetrator before the perpetrator realises that the police are investigating.

The difficulty with this approach is that you may have a duty of care to apply for deputyship in the interim to protect the assets from being further dissipated by the perpetrator. If the perpetrator is a deputy or attorney, the OPG will want to launch an investigation.

> **TIP**
>
> In a fraud situation you are in a removal of attorney application position. Attorneys under an LPA are expected to act in the Donor's best interests at all times and follow the Code of Practice. If they cannot be trusted to act in the Donor's best interests, case law has shown that the Public Guardian and the Court of Protection will intervene and the LPA may be revoked and cancelled in some circumstances. But you need to make sure that you have the evidence to go down this route.

Excessive gifts[60]

Whilst attorneys can make gifts to people related to or connected with the donor, including themselves, these gifts should only be on customary occasions (for example birthdays, Christmas, etc) and should not be unreasonably large. The gifts should also not be disproportionate to the pattern of giving the donor did when they had capacity.

One of the consequences of an Attorney exceeding his or her authority could be realised at the time of dealing with an individual's estate. At that time, the Revenue will ask to see a copy of the Power of Attorney and will then look to see what gifts have been declared being made during the last seven years.

If the Donor had lost capacity and gifts were continuing to be made the Revenue may argue that the gifts are void and the value should be aggregated to the estate, with a result that the additional Inheritance Tax will be payable, plus there will be the potential for interest and penalties.

Matters could be even worse if there is evidence that there is a general deficiency in a Donor's funds because an Attorney has been withdrawing excessive sums from his or her account. In the case of R v TJC [2015] EWCA the Court of Appeal (Criminal Division) held that in such circumstances the Attorney would be guilty of an abuse of position under Section 4 of the Fraud Act 2006.

In this case the withdrawals being made by the Attorney were unreasonably high given the needs of the Donor. The conclusion was that the Attorney could not have been acting honesty when managing the affairs of the Donor.

---

60 There is some useful guidance here: https://www.gov.uk/government/publications/public-guardian-practice-note-gifts/public-guardian-practice-note-pn7-giving-gifts-web-version

It is easy to believe that as an Attorney, you are, in effect, standing in the same shoes as the Donor, and can act as he or she would do.

It is important for the Attorneys to remember that they must always act in the best interest of the Donor.

An attorney needs to take particular care if he or she is thinking of accepting a gift from the person's estate.

If one does accept a gift, the Court of Protection can look carefully at whether the person had capacity and may decide the attorney went beyond authority.

In the case of PG v DH [2014] EWCOP 15 (15 July 2014), Senior Judge Lush decided that the facts pointed to the 'donor' of a power of attorney (the legal term for the person who made it) lacking capacity to agree to a loan her son had taken out on her property. In this case, the donor's loan counted as a gift to her son.

Senior Judge Lush commented that:

> *"... even if VH had the capacity to make the gift, it was reprehensible [wrong] of him [the attorney] to have accepted it... and shows that when faced with a conflict between his interests and his mother's, he would place his own interests first."*

Loan applications or credit cards taken out in the donor's name

This could raise concerns about potential misuse of the attorney's powers, particularly if the donor does not benefit from the loans or credit cards. In Re Harcourt,[61] Mrs Harcourt's daughter became an attorney after her mother lost capacity.

---

61 Re Harcourt [2012] WTLR 1779

Suspicions were raised when the care home manager became aware of letters about bank loans and credit card applications being taken out by the daughter in her mother's name. The matter was consequently investigated, and it was revealed that the daughter had abused her powers of attorney to make personal financial gains.

High risk investments or investment in a business the attorney owns or has an interest in

The issue of investments was considered in the Court of Protection No. 12228697 Buckley v The Public Guardian.

The Senior Judge in the Court of Protection, Denzil Lush, stated that he wished to use this case to discuss the responsibilities of an attorney acting under an LPA when investing donor's funds.

> "There are two common misconceptions when it comes to investments. The first is that attorneys acting under an LPA can do whatever they like with the donors' funds. And the second is that attorneys can do whatever the donors could – or would – have done personally, if they had the capacity to manage their property and financial affairs."
>
> "Managing your own money is one thing. Managing someone else's money is an entirely different matter."

Cancel the LPA

If the donor has sufficient capacity, they can cancel the LPA by signing a Deed of Revocation and notifying the attorney.

If the donor does not have capacity, you can contact the Office of the Public Guardian in the first instance and ask them to investigate the concerns.

If you have sufficient evidence regarding the abuse, you could make an application to the Court of Protection for an order that the LPA is cancelled and a deputy is instead appointed to manage the vulnerable person's finances. It is advisable to seek legal advice before court proceedings are started."

Applications for permission to make gifts

Attorneys and deputies have limited powers by which they can make gifts, or an application can be made to the Court of Protection for approval of a more substantial gift.

Applications for permission for property transactions

Attorneys and deputies may have the authority to sell the property belonging to the person lacking capacity. However, on occasion an application to the Court of Protection is required to obtain approval for such a transaction. This could be because the sale is at below market value or because a family member wants to buy it.

Costs Within Court of Protection

The Court of Protection operates via its own rules, namely the Court of Protection Rules 2017. Rule 19 contains the key costs provisions, and the accompanying practice direction sets out the way in which cost claims would ordinarily be dealt with by the Court. The CPR does not apply automatically, although, in certain circumstances, various provisions from the CPR can be implemented.

Essentially, these are the key aspects of the way in which costs are dealt with in the Court of Protection:

- In proceedings which concern the property and financial affairs of a protected party, the legal costs of the parties will usually be met from the protected party's resources, subject to assessment;

- In health and welfare proceedings, all parties are usually expected to pay their own costs, and there is no automatic recovery from any other party, including from the protected party;

- The Court has discretion in all cases to allow/disallow costs recovery if the circumstances are exceptional or if the behaviour of one or more of the parties merits an alternative order.

Resolving Evidential Problems of Fraud

- It is often difficult to find specific evidence in these circumstances as to what the attorney has done with missing funds, and it is useful to know that even when it comes to meeting the onerous burden of proving fraud, it is not always necessary to determine exactly what the funds have been spent on.

- This is demonstrated by the case of R v TJC [2015] EWCA Crim 1276. In this case it was held that it is possible to bring a charge against an attorney if there is 'abuse of position' under Section 4 of the Fraud Act 2006.[62] The Court held that the circumstances would need to show that there is evidence of a general deficiency in the donor's funds as a result of withdrawals made by an attorney. In this case, the Court of Appeal held that it was not necessary for the prosecution to present evidence of specific fraudulent transactions, i.e. identifying each withdrawal against expenditure. What was sufficient in this case was demonstrating

---

62 In an initial letter of claim, threatening criminal proceedings and quoting legislation and case law can be a useful step but you must ensure that you have evidence to back it up and please be careful and not over-aggressive.

that the total value of withdrawals by the Attorney (totalling approximately £75,000), exceeded the reasonable sums that would have been incurred over specific periods in providing for the donor given their needs. In this case, although it was accepted that some of the funds were spent on the donor, the Attorney had been spending "sums to such a degree and in such high quantities in certain given months that she could not possibly have been acting honestly".

- In general, where there is suspected financial abuse by an attorney, the Office of the Public Guardian ("OPG") should be informed immediately.

Separate Legal Proceedings

It may also be appropriate to consider an action for breach of fiduciary duty, negligence, or a claim for restitution on the basis that the attorney has been unjustly enriched through misuse of the donor's funds. This typically happens after the Deceased has died and you are involved in an action for someone who has suffered financial loss due to the conduct of the attorney though legal action may be brought both in the lifetime of the victim and after their death.

There are a variety of civil actions that may be appropriate in circumstances of financial abuse including:

- Set aside on the grounds of lack of capacity: The test for mental capacity for an inter vivos gift has been stated in Re Beaney [1978] 2 All ER 595 as follows: "the principle is that the mental capacity required by the law in respect of any instrument is relative to the particular transaction which is being effected by means of the instrument, and may be described as the capacity to understand the nature of that transaction when it is explained."

- Breach of fiduciary duty / breach of trust: in circumstances where a person has assumed a responsibility for assisting another with their finances pursuant to a power of attorney or as a court appointed deputy, the courts have recognised that a fiduciary relationship arises.[63]

- Unduc influence: Undue influence is an equitable doctrine which provides that transactions (including gifts and contracts) may be set aside in circumstances where the transaction has been procured by conduct, which, whilst falling short of actual fraud, consists of the exercise of an unfair advantage, typically by a party in a position of power, influence or trust, over the other party to the transaction. Please see relevant chapter.

- Morally culpable behaviour: The weakness of one party has to have been exploited by the other in some morally culpable manner. Overreaching or oppressive result: The resulting transaction must be not merely hard or improvident, but overreaching or oppressive.

Approaching Cases

Attorneys under an LPA are expected to act in the Donor's best interests always and follow the Code of Practice. If they cannot be trusted to act in the Donor's best interests, recent case law has shown that the Public

---

63 No period of limitation applies to an action by a beneficiary under a trust in respect of any fraud or fraudulent breach of trust to which the trustee was a party, or to recover from the trustee trust property (or the proceeds of trust property) in the possession of the trustee (section 21(1) of the Limitation Act 1980) (a time limit of six years will apply in the case of non-fraudulent breaches of trust or fiduciary duty).

Guardian and the Court of Protection will intervene, and the LPA may be revoked and cancelled in some circumstances.

A very useful piece of legislation is the Mentality Capacity Code and as a lawyer I like to remind errant attorneys of their breaches.

> *Principles and best interests*
>
> *7.53 Attorneys must act in accordance with the Act's statutory principles (section 1) and in the best interests of the donor (the steps for working out best interests are set out in section 4). In particular, attorneys must consider whether the donor has capacity to make the decision for themselves. If not, they should consider whether the donor is likely to regain capacity to make the decision in the future. If so, it may be possible to delay the decision until the donor can make it.*
>
> *What are an attorney's other duties?*
>
> *7.58 An attorney appointed under an LPA is acting as the chosen agent of the donor and therefore, under the law of agency, the attorney has certain duties towards the donor. An attorney takes on a role which carries a great deal of power, which they must use carefully and responsibly. They have a duty to:*
>
> - *apply certain standards of care and skill (duty of care) when making decisions*
> - *carry out the donor's instructions*
> - *not take advantage of their position and not benefit themselves, but benefit the donor (fiduciary duty)*
> - *not delegate decisions, unless authorised to do so*
> - *act in good faith*

- *respect confidentiality*
- *comply with the directions of the Court of Protection*
- *not give up the role without telling the donor and the court.*

In relation to property and affairs LPAs, they have a duty to:

- *keep accounts*
- *Keep the donor's money and property separate from their own.*

Duty of care

7.59 'Duty of care' means applying a certain standard of care and skill – depending on whether the attorney is paid for their services or holds relevant professional qualifications.

- *Attorneys who are not being paid must apply the same care, skill and diligence they would use to make decisions about their own life. An attorney who claims to have particular skills or qualifications must show greater skill in those particular areas than someone who does not make such claims.*
- *If attorneys are being paid for their services, they should demonstrate a higher degree of care and skill.*
- *Attorneys who undertake their duties in the course of their professional work (such as solicitors or corporate trustees) must display professional competence and follow their profession's rules and standards.*

Mental Capacity Act Code of Practice Fiduciary duty

7.60 A fiduciary duty means attorneys must not take advantage of their position. Nor should they put themselves in a position where their personal interests' conflict with their duties. They also must not allow any other influences to affect the way in which they act as an attorney. Decisions should always benefit the donor, and not the attorney. Attorneys must not profit or get any personal benefit from their position, apart from receiving gifts where the Act allows it, whether or not it is at the donor's expense.

Duty of good faith

7.63 Acting in good faith means acting with honesty and integrity. For example, an attorney must try to make sure that their decisions do not go against a decision the donor made while they still had capacity

(unless it would be in the donor's best interests to do so).

MORE BOOKS BY LAW BRIEF PUBLISHING

A selection of our other titles available now:-

'A Practical Guide to Probation Breaches and Other Applications' by Mark Thomas
'A Practical Guide to Remarriage and Divorce' by Cordelia Williams & Claire Howard
'A Practical Guide to Privacy, Transparency, Reporting Restrictions and Closed Proceedings in the Court of Protection' by Laura Mannering
'Beaumont on Barristers – A Guide to Defending Disciplinary Proceedings (Second Edition)' by Marc Beaumont
'A Practical Guide to Payments for Environmental Services' by Ben Sharples
'A Practical Guide to the Law of Pregnancy and Maternity at Work' by Rebecca Thomas
'A Practical Guide to Redundancy – Second Edition' by Philip Hyland & Collette Moore
'A Practical Guide to International Issues for Scottish Family Lawyers' by Susie Mountain, Donna McKay, Ken MacDonald
'A Practical Guide to the Law on Deprivation of Liberty' by Ben Troke
'A Practical Guide to Rights over Airspace and Subsoil – Second Edition' by Daniel Gatty
'A Practical Guide to the Law in Relation to Inquests' by Ramya Nagesh
'A Practical Guide to the Construction and Rectification of Wills and Trust Instruments (Second Edition)' by Edward Hewitt
'A Practical Guide to Data Protection in Social Housing' by Clare Paterson
'A Practical Guide to Spousal Maintenance – Second Edition' by Liz Cowell
'A Practical Guide to International Parental Child Abduction Law (England and Wales)' by Dr Onyója Momoh
'A Practical Guide to Deprivation of British Citizenship' by Sean Ell
'A Practical Guide to Commercial Property Service Charges' by Rachel Garton
'A Practical Guide to Clinical Negligence – Third Edition' by Geoffrey Simpson-Scott (Geoff)
'A Practical Guide to the Rights of Grandparents in Children Proceedings – Second Edition' by Stuart Barlow

'The Electronic Communications Code: A Practical Guide – Second Edition' by Kerry Bretherton KC, James Castle, Mark Loveday
'A Practical Guide to the Independent School Standards – September 2023 Edition' by Sarah McKimm
'A Practical Guide to Estate Administration and Crypto Assets' by Richard Marshall
'A Practical Guide to Parental Alienation in Private and Public Law Children Cases' by Sam King QC & Frankie Shama
'Contested Heritage – Removing Art from Land and Historic Buildings' by Richard Harwood QC, Catherine Dobson, David Sawtell
'The Limits of Separate Legal Personality: When Those Running a Company Can Be Held Personally Liable for Losses Caused to Third Parties Outside of the Company' by Dr Mike Wilkinson
'A Practical Guide to Transgender Law' by Robin Moira White & Nicola Newbegin
'A Practical Guide to 'Stranded Spouses' in Family Law' by Mani Singh Basi
'A Practical Guide to Residential Freehold Conveyancing' by Lorraine Richardson
'A Practical Guide to Pensions on Divorce for Lawyers' by Bryan Scant
'A Practical Guide to Challenging Sham Marriage Allegations in Immigration Law' by Priya Solanki
'A Practical Guide to Digital Communications Evidence in Criminal Law' by Sam Willis
'A Practical Guide to Legal Rights in Scotland' by Sarah-Jane Macdonald
'A Practical Guide to New Build Conveyancing' by Paul Sams & Rebecca East
'A Practical Guide to Inherited Wealth on Divorce' by Hayley Trim
'A Practical Guide to Practice Direction 12J and Domestic Abuse in Private Law Children Proceedings' by Rebecca Cross & Malvika Jaganmohan
'A Practical Guide to Confiscation and Restraint' by Narita Bahra QC, John Carl Townsend, David Winch
'A Practical Guide to the Law of Forests in Scotland' by Philip Buchan
'A Practical Guide to Health and Medical Cases in Immigration Law' by Rebecca Chapman & Miranda Butler
'A Practical Guide to Bad Character Evidence for Criminal Practitioners by Aparna Rao
'A Practical Guide to Extradition Law post-Brexit' by Myles Grandison et al
'A Practical Guide to Hoarding and Mental Health for Housing Lawyers' by Rachel Coyle

'Stephens on Contractual Indemnities' by Richard Stephens
'A Practical Guide to the EU Succession Regulation' by Richard Frimston
'A Practical Guide to Solicitor and Client Costs – Second Edition' by Robin Dunne
'Constructive Dismissal – Practice Pointers and Principles' by Benjimin Burgher
'A Practical Guide to Religion and Belief Discrimination Claims in the Workplace' by Kashif Ali
'A Practical Guide to the Law of Medical Treatment Decisions' by Ben Troke
'Fundamental Dishonesty and QOCS in Personal Injury Proceedings: Law and Practice' by Jake Rowley
'A Practical Guide to the Law in Relation to School Exclusions' by Charlotte Hadfield & Alice de Coverley
'A Practical Guide to Divorce for the Silver Separators' by Karin Walker
'The Right to be Forgotten – The Law and Practical Issues' by Melissa Stock
'A Practical Guide to Planning Law and Rights of Way in National Parks, the Broads and AONBs' by James Maurici QC, James Neill et al
'A Practical Guide to Election Law' by Tom Tabori
'A Practical Guide to the Law in Relation to Surrogacy' by Andrew Powell
'A Practical Guide to Claims Arising from Fatal Accidents – Second Edition' by James Patience
'A Practical Guide to Asbestos Claims' by Jonathan Owen & Gareth McAloon
'A Practical Guide to Stamp Duty Land Tax in England and Northern Ireland' by Suzanne O'Hara
'A Practical Guide to the Law of Farming Partnerships' by Philip Whitcomb
'A Practical Guide to the Law of Unlawful Eviction and Harassment – Second Edition' by Stephanie Lovegrove
'A Practical Guide to Costs in Personal Injury Claims – Second Edition' by Matthew Hoe
'A Practical Guide to the General Data Protection Regulation (GDPR) – Second Edition' by Keith Markham
'A Practical Guide to Working with Litigants in Person and McKenzie Friends in Family Cases' by Stuart Barlow
'Protecting Unregistered Brands: A Practical Guide to the Law of Passing Off' by Lorna Brazell
'A Practical Guide to Secondary Liability and Joint Enterprise Post-Jogee' by Joanne Cecil & James Mehigan

'A Practical Guide to the Pre-Action RTA Claims Protocol for Personal Injury Lawyers' by Antonia Ford
'A Practical Guide to Neighbour Disputes and the Law' by Alexander Walsh
'A Practical Guide to Coercive Control for Legal Practitioners and Victims' by Rachel Horman
'A Practical Guide to the Law of Driverless Cars – Second Edition'
by Alex Glassbrook, Emma Northey & Scarlett Milligan
'A Practical Guide to TOLATA Claims' by Greg Williams
'A Practical Guide to Elderly Law – Second Edition' by Justin Patten
'A Practical Guide to Responding to Housing Disrepair and Unfitness Claims' by Iain Wightwick
'A Practical Guide to the Law of Bullying and Harassment in the Workplace' by Philip Hyland
'How to Be a Freelance Solicitor: A Practical Guide to the SRA-Regulated Freelance Solicitor Model' by Paul Bennett
'A Practical Guide to Prison Injury Claims' by Malcolm Johnson
'A Practical Guide to Advising Clients at the Police Station' by Colin Stephen McKeown-Beaumont
'A Practical Guide to Antisocial Behaviour Injunctions – Second Edition' by Iain Wightwick
'Practical Mediation: A Guide for Mediators, Advocates, Advisers, Lawyers, and Students in Civil, Commercial, Business, Property, Workplace, and Employment Cases' by Jonathan Dingle with John Sephton
'The Mini-Pupillage Workbook' by David Boyle
'A Practical Guide to Crofting Law' by Brian Inkster
'A Practical Guide to the Law of Domain Names and Cybersquatting' by Andrew Clemson
'A Practical Guide to the Law of Gender Pay Gap Reporting' by Harini Iyengar
'NHS Whistleblowing and the Law' by Joseph England
'Employment Law and the Gig Economy' by Nigel Mackay & Annie Powell
'A Practical Guide to Noise Induced Hearing Loss (NIHL) Claims' by Andrew Mckie, Ian Skeate, Gareth McAloon
'An Introduction to Beauty Negligence Claims – A Practical Guide for the Personal Injury Practitioner' by Greg Almond
'Intercompany Agreements for Transfer Pricing Compliance' by Paul Sutton
'Zen and the Art of Mediation' by Martin Plowman
'A Practical Guide to Adoption for Family Lawyers' by Graham Pegg

'A Practical Guide to Industrial Disease Claims' by Andrew Mckie & Ian Skeate
'A Practical Guide to Conducting a Sheriff Court Proof' by Andrew Stevenson
'A Practical Guide to Vicarious Liability' by Mariel Irvine
'A Practical Guide to Applications for Landlord's Consent and Variation of Leases' by Mark Shelton
'A Practical Guide to Relief from Sanctions Post-Mitchell and Denton' by Peter Causton
'A Practical Guide to Equity Release for Advisors' by Paul Sams
'A Practical Guide to Financial Services Claims' by Chris Hegarty
'A Practical Guide to Financial Ombudsman Service Claims' by Adam Temple & Robert Scrivenor
'A Practical Guide to Running Housing Disrepair and Cavity Wall Claims – Second Edition' by Andrew Mckie & Ian Skeate
'A Practical Guide to Holiday Sickness Claims – Second Edition' by Andrew Mckie & Ian Skeate
'Arguments and Tactics for Personal Injury and Clinical Negligence Claims' by Dorian Williams
'A Practical Guide to Drone Law' by Rufus Ballaster, Andrew Firman, Eleanor Clot
'On Experts: CPR35 for Lawyers and Experts' by David Boyle
'An Introduction to Personal Injury Law' by David Boyle

These books and more are available to order online direct from the publisher at www.lawbriefpublishing.com, where you can also read free sample chapters. For any queries, call us on 0844 587 2383 or email us at mail@lawbriefpublishing.com.

Our books are all generally in stock at www.amazon.co.uk with free next day delivery for Prime members, and at good legal bookshops such as Wildy & Sons.

We are regularly launching new books in our series of practical day-to-day practitioners' guides. Visit our website and join our free newsletter to be kept informed and to receive special offers, free chapters, etc.

You can also follow us on Twitter at www.twitter.com/lawbriefpub.

www.ingramcontent.com/pod-product-compliance
Ingram Content Group UK Ltd.
Pitfield, Milton Keynes, MK11 3LW, UK
UKHW021239300926
15471UKWH00013B/685